Sell your books at World of Books!

Go to sell.worldofbooks.com and get an instant price quote. We even pay the shipping - see our old books are worth

CANADIAN PACIFIC STEAM
In Color

VOL. 2: MONTREAL & WEST

KEVIN J. HOLLAND

Copyright © 2006
Morning Sun Books, Inc.
All rights reserved. This book may not be reproduced in part or in whole without written permission from the publisher, except in the case of brief quotations or reproduction of the cover for the purposes of review.

Robert J. Yanosey, President

To access our full library *In Color* visit us at
www.morningsunbooks.com

Published by
Morning Sun Books, Inc.
9 Pheasant Lane
Scotch Plains, NJ 07076

Printed in Korea

Library of Congress
Control Number: 2005928876

First Printing
ISBN 1-58248-182-2

Design and production by
Kevin J. Holland
type&DESIGN
Burlington, Ontario

CONTENTS

INTRODUCTION	3
MONTREAL	12
ONTARIO	54
SMITHS FALLS	56
GUELPH JUNCTION	64
HAMILTON	82
PRAIRIES	90
MANITOBA	92
SASKATCHEWAN	100
MOUNTAINS	106
MAIN LINE	108
CROWSNEST	116
KETTLE VALLEY	122

ACKNOWLEDGMENTS

When publisher Bob Yanosey broached the idea of producing a multi-volume review of Canadian National and Canadian Pacific steam locomotives, one look at the several hundred slides forming the core of the effort revealed a spectacular body of work that, with very few exceptions, was previously unpublished. Almost as appealing as the collection of distinctive and colorful subjects was the perspective of the photographers. All Americans, their periodic trips north to Canada from the late 1940s into 1960 generated a photographic record capturing concentrated periods of railway operation at a remarkable, yet representative, range of locations across the country. The looming trip home, undoubtedly, was incentive to record as much Canadian activity as possible, including trains toward which "the locals," less pressed for time, might turn a blind eye. Not surprisingly, with most of these U.S. fans living in the Northeast and upper Midwest, and nearby eastern Canada offering an accessible sampling of urban and rural steam operations right to the end, activity in Ontario and Quebec was the object of their most frequent attention. It is hoped that the eastern weighting of this volume will be offset by the inclusion of rare views along British Columbia's early-to-dieselize Kootenay and Kettle Valley Divisions, as well as images from a 1949 mainline trip through the Rockies to Vancouver.

Readers of this volume and its companion are indebted to the following photographers for their perseverance and skill: Dr. Howard Blackburn, Robert F. Collins, George Dimond, Sandy Goodrick, Emery Gulash, Preston Johnson, and William J. McChesney. Images not otherwise credited are from the author's collection.

Once again I extend my heartfelt appreciation to Bob Yanosey, for entrusting me with the compilation and production of this project and for allowing its presentation in two volumes. Through Morning Sun Books, Bob has preserved the increasingly fragile visual record created by an unparalleled fraternity of photographers. Without their combined efforts, it is a record that would otherwise be lost.

CANADIAN PACIFIC IN TRANSITION

With Canada's economy and transportation network struggling to find a "new normal" in the postwar 1940s, Canadian Pacific was poised to enter what, in many respects, was the apogee of its globe-girdling importance. "Canadian Pacific Spans the World," proclaimed a modernized crest merging a buoyant script company name with the revival of a long-dormant CPR mascot, the industrious beaver.

In 1947, the CPR controlled over 17,000 miles of track in Canada and a further 3,796 in the United States. It maintained over 77,000 freight cars, 2,801 passenger cars and, tellingly, 184 snowplows (including six rotaries). The company reached beyond Canada's shores with a burgeoning airline, which that July commenced trans-Pacific service with a pioneering route to Australia. A widely respected steamship subsidiary, still recovering from wartime tonnage losses, nonetheless had resumed regular transatlantic passenger and freight service, and also maintained operations on the Great Lakes. Bolstering this far-flung empire at home were 14 large hotels and a quartet of holiday camps, which combined to make Canadian Pacific the owner and operator of Canada's largest hotel chain.

Conservative modernism might best describe the Canadian Pacific Railway's early postwar mission, which through the end of the 1940s saw the company content to merely dabble with dieselization.

EVOLUTION, NOT REVOLUTION

Gradual transitions had marked the previous two decades of CPR motive power development, after Henry Bowen had risen to the position of motive power chief in 1928. One of Bowen's first decisions was giving the 4-6-4 Hudson wheel arrangement the nod as his preferred heavy passenger power, turning his back on a pair of K1 Northerns recently introduced for that role by his predecessor, Charles Temple. Destined to be the CPR's only 4-8-4s, the

Canadian Pacific augmented its basic black steam locomotive livery in May 1935, when maroon accent panels were applied to the tender, cab, and running boards of H1a Hudson No. 2802. Later that year, other engines in passenger service began to receive the treatment. Maroon (called Tuscan red by the CPR) had long been the color used on the railway's passenger rolling stock, and a 1933 North American visit by the similarly painted *Royal Scot* may have inspired the CPR to extend the coloration to its passenger locomotives. Until 1948, lettering and striping on passenger power was applied in gold leaf; after that, the yellow paint previously employed on freight power was used. H1b No. 2811 was at Chalk River, Ontario, on August 28, 1958.
ROBERT F. COLLINS, MORNING SUN BOOKS COLLECTION

This map of the CPR's main lines appeared in a 1939 folder describing the just-completed Canadian tour of Their Majesties King George VI and Queen Elizabeth, and promoting the visit to that summer's New York World's Fair of the specially painted locomotive that led their train on CPR rails, H1d Hudson No. 2850. The King and Queen traveled west from Quebec City to Vancouver, and crossed the Atlantic in both directions, in the care of Canadian Pacific.
AUTHOR'S COLLECTION

pair was considered by Temple's replacement as too heavy for widespread use. The H1 Hudson design introduced by Bowen in 1929, meanwhile, proved ideally suited to the railway's heavy passenger assignments in all but the steepest territory. The CPR had employed 4-6-2 Pacifics since 1906, and Bowen saw sufficient versatility and utility in that wheel arrangement that he continued buying them, suitably modernized, until 1948. So convinced was Bowen of steam's superiority over diesel that he oversaw the acquisition of 430 steam locomotives, including 224 Pacifics, 69 Mikados, 65 Hudsons, 37 Selkirks, and 25 Jubilees. The final new CPR steam locomotive, semi-streamlined T1c 2-10-4 No. 5935, arrived in March 1949.

Even against this backdrop, however, Bowen did consider the utility of the diesel in specific applications. The railway's first such locomotive purchase, an end-cab diesel-electric switcher delivered as No. 7000 in 1937, was evaluated for several years before being sold off, but paved the way for additional yard units during the war.

D10g 4-6-0 No. 946 was an October 1911 product of the Montreal Locomotive Works (MLW). The D10 was the largest single class on the CPR's all-time steam roster, and among the longest-lived. Near its 48th birthday, No. 946 led an excursion in October 1959.
AUTHOR'S COLLECTION

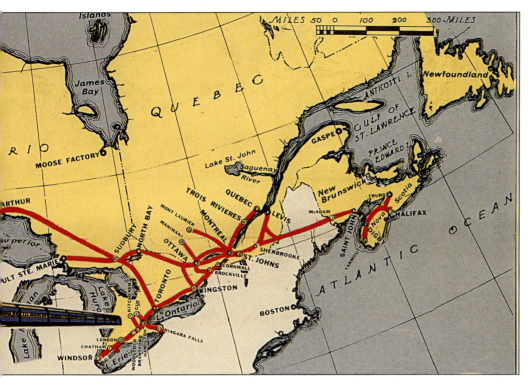

Bowen was also responsible for the cosmetic evolution of CPR steam when he introduced a distinctive semi-streamlined appearance. First employed on the quintet of speedy 4-4-4 F2a Jubilees (Nos. 3000-3004) in 1936, this "family look" was also employed on subsequent Hudsons, smaller F1a Jubilees, and the T2b and T2c 2-10-4 Selkirks. A similar but less sleek treatment showed up on Mikados and heavy Pacifics built after the late 1930s.

PASSING THE TORCH

The CPR's all-time steam roster numbered almost 3,300 locomotives of 23 wheel arrangements, from diminutive 0-4-0s and 4-4-0s to ponderous 0-6-6-0s and 2-10-4s. Over 1,000 of these locomotives were built by the CPR at its Montreal shops. The most numerous wheel arrangement on the railway's all-time roster was the 4-6-0 Ten-wheeler, with 971 representatives. Fully 502 of these belonged to a single class, the ubiquitous D10. Despite their advancing years, and Bowen's desire to see them supplanted wherever possible

Shunning the "revolutionary" steam streamlining emerging in Europe and the U.S., in the mid-1930s the CPR's Henry Bowen instead opted for a more "evolutionary" cleaning-up of the locomotive's characteristic lines. F1a Jubilee No. 2929, at Montreal on August 29, 1958, modeled the CPR's semi-streamlined family look. The "stovepipe" exhaust stack was a latter-day modification eliminating the original low-profile stack fairing in an attempt to prevent smoke from obscuring the crew's view.
ROBERT F. COLLINS, MORNING SUN BOOKS COLLECTION

ABOVE: M4g 2-8-0 No. 3524, at North Bay, Ont., in August 1958, was built by Baldwin in June 1907 as No. 1724. A systemwide renumbering begun in 1912 gave the Consolidation the identity it would keep until retirement and scrapping in January 1960.

BELOW: Henry Bowen's G5 Pacific design of 1944 may have looked antiquated, but features like welded domeless boilers, mechanical lubrication, HT-1 stokers, and electro-mechanical blowdown were thoroughly modern. G5c No. 1266 was built in January 1947.
BOTH, ROBERT F. COLLINS, MORNING SUN BOOKS COLLECTION

after the early 1940s by his modern G5 Pacifics, D10s remained plentiful across the railway until the end of steam.

In 1950, the year after Bowen's retirement, Canadian Pacific's locomotive roster comprised 1,718 steam locomotives. Just over 200 of these were oil-fired, for service on the railway's "Western Lines," where they worked in concert with about 700 coal burners. Consuming a different form of oil that year were 132 CPR diesels, 49 of which were assigned to the Western Lines.

The tide had turned as far as CPR motive power policy was concerned. A new generation of managers under recently appointed President & Chairman W. M. Neal was developing systematic plans to implement complete dieselization.

Initially, a regional approach was adopted, with relatively self-contained operations on Vancouver Island (the CPR's Esquimalt & Nanaimo subsidiary), Vermont (from Wells River north to Montreal), northern Ontario (Cartier to Ft. William on the Schreiber Division), and British Columbia's Kootenay and Kettle Valley Divisions dieselized between early 1949 and the end of 1953.

The mid-1950s saw CPR dieselization progress rapidly, largely at the urging of Vice-President (soon to be CPR president) N. R. "Buck" Crump, the man then also driving the creation of a state-of-the-art cross-country streamlined passenger train, *The Canadian* (see sidebar opposite). This diesel-powered Budd domeliner was, literally, a shining example of Crump's desire to conclude mainline dieselization on a train-by-train basis.

Even as Canadian Pacific dieselization accelerated towards completion, a final target date was hard to pin down; some analysts thought steam would linger until the mid-1960s. A late-1950s general economic downturn, though, combined with the localized impact of the newly opened St. Lawrence Seaway siphoning off traffic, meant that enough diesels were on hand by early 1960 to handle the reduced traffic levels and permit retirement of the last active CPR steam locomotives, which by then had gravitated to Montreal.

THE CANADIAN

One of the most dazzling elements of Canadian Pacific's postwar metamorphosis debuted on April 24, 1955, when *The Canadian* made its inaugural departures from Montreal, Toronto, and Vancouver. Progressive even beyond its then state-of-the-art Budd rolling stock and rich decor, *The Canadian* was intended from its inception to be an all-diesel operation. The motive power choice was practical as much as it was progressive, since the diesels' rapid acceleration combined with the Budd cars' disk brakes permitted upwards of 16 hours to be slashed from the CPR's then-fastest transcontinental schedule. General Motors F-units were the motive power of choice for *The Canadian*, with Alco-design cab and booster units built by MLW also employed. Steam is known to have led *The Canadian* on a handful of occasions, as late as 1959, when the train's assigned diesels failed.

The Canadian introduced stainless steel equipment, domes, streamlined observation cars and a host of other milestones to revenue service on a Canadian railway. Until well along in the new train's development, it was to have been called *The Royal Canadian*. Calendars were even printed with the name, which for eleventh-hour political and pragmatic reasons was truncated to *The Canadian* shortly before the train's inauguration.

With an interior decor celebrating Canada's history and scenic variety, *The Canadian* was promoted by the CPR as having almost as much appeal as the scenery through which it traveled. To this end, original murals and other art was commissioned from some of Canada's leading artists, and car names were carefully selected to honor historic figures and locales. Two series of sleeping cars were built for the train; the *Manor* series honored Canadians of British origin, while the *Chateau* series recognized those of French descent. Reflecting the times, Native personages were overlooked, although stereotypical "Indian" imagery was employed in some of *The Canadian's* 1950s promotional material. Dining cars were named to celebrate public rooms in Canadian Pacific hotels, while *The Canadian's* signature dome-sleeper-observation cars (near duplicates of those built earlier for the *California Zephyr*) were named in the *Park* series after 18 national and provincial parks located along the Canadian Pacific route. Notably but understandably absent from the latter series was a car named in honor of Jasper National Park, a spectacular Rockies destination which had the distinction of being traversed by rival Canadian National, and was also the site of the CNR's famed Jasper Park Lodge.

In addition to the observation and dome space provided in the *Park* cars, passengers could view the passing countryside from another 24-seat "Scenic Dome" in the 18 "Skyline" buffet-coaches built for service on *The Canadian* and its selectively upgraded running mate, the *Dominion*.

Both trains provided double-daily cross-Canada schedules until the *Dominion's* 1965 discontinuance, and again in the summer of 1967, Canada's centennial year, when the latter train was resurrected as the *Expo Limited* to take advantage of a traffic surge created by the Expo67 world's fair in Montreal.

ABOVE: The CPR spared no expense in promoting its new domeliner, with imagery invariably showing the train in the Rockies. AUTHOR'S COLLECTION

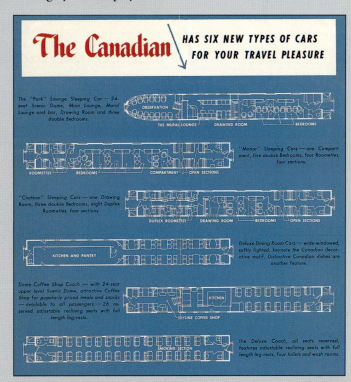

Suburban trains running to and from Montreal's Windsor Station behind Pacifics and Hudsons (the latter both "standard" and semi-streamlined) were Canadian Pacific steam's final regular-service assignment, and the last of these ran in June 1960.

Rather than being summarily retired, a few of the locomotives from this pool, based at Glen Yard in Westmount, just west of Windsor Station, were stored with the possibility of a return to service. They were fleetingly returned to steam for heating-plant duty at Glen Yard in February and March 1961, providing steam to the facility while its permanent plant underwent maintenance. When engines in this service, among them H1b No. 2816, needed mechanical attention, they ran light to St. Luc Yard's roundhouse and back to "the Glen" under their own steam.

TOP: Progress often comes at a price. Nearly 100 scrapped CPR steam locomotives are represented by their salvaged bells in this 1960 view at Montreal's Angus Shops.
DR. HOWARD BLACKBURN, MORNING SUN BOOKS COLLECTION

MIDDLE: Stack capped, and headlight and cab windows boarded up, D10e No. 807 had run its last miles under steam when it was photographed at Winnipeg in October 1958. This engine had spent its last active years assigned to the CPR's Western Lines (west of Lake Superior), based in Estevan, Saskatchewan.
AUTHOR'S COLLECTION

BOTTOM: Consigned to a similar fate, Jubilee No. 3004 has had its stack and headlight shrouded in this March 29, 1958, view at Montreal. None of the F2a speedsters avoided scrapping, although two of the smaller and more numerous F1a 4-4-4 design were saved.
ROBERT F. COLLINS, MORNING SUN BOOKS COLLECTION

 # CPR STEAM ROSTER SUMMARY: 1950–1960

Series	Type	Class	Notes
6-159	4-4-0	A	Only Nos. 29, 136, and 144 were active through the 1950s.
417-492	4-6-0	D4g	
520-538	4-6-0	D6b	
560-597	4-6-0	D9c	
600-1111	4-6-0	D10	Most numerous steam locomotive class on all-time CPR roster.
1200-1301	4-6-2	G5	No. 1201 last steam locomotive built by the CPR (Angus Shops, Montreal, June 1944).
2200-2238	4-6-2	G1	
2500-2665	4-6-2	G2	
2300-2472	4-6-2	G3	
2700-2717	4-6-2	G4	
2800-2865	4-6-4	H1	Nos. 2820-2865 semi-streamlined, known as "Royal Hudsons."
2900-2929	4-4-4	F1a	Semi-streamlined.
3000-3004	4-4-4	F2a	Semi-streamlined.
3100-3101	4-8-4	K1	
3350-3391	2-8-0	M3	
3400-3565	2-8-0	M4	
3600-3760	2-8-0	N2	
3800-3960	2-8-0	N3	
5100-5264	2-8-2	P1	
5300-5473	2-8-2	P2	
5750-5755	2-10-0	R2	
5756-5790	2-10-0	R3	
5800-5814	2-10-2	S2a	
5900-5935	2-10-4	T1	Nos. 5920-5935 semi-streamlined. No. 5935 last steam locomotive built for CPR (MLW, March 1949).
6209-6259	0-6-0	U3d	
6260-6304	0-6-0	U3e	
6900-6913	0-8-0	V3	
6920-6949	0-8-0	V4a	
6960-6968	0-8-0	V5a	Re# from V5a 6600-6609 (6603 scrapped) during 1956-57 to clear roster slot for MLW S-3 diesel switchers.
6950-6952	0-10-0	W1a	

Not all classes shown. Some members of series shown were retired pre-1950. Source: Canadian Pacific Railway mechanical records.

LIVING MEMORIES

The relatively late date of final CPR dieselization meant that preservationists existed in sufficient numbers, and with sufficient resources, to ensure the sparing of a number of otherwise scrapper-bound Canadian Pacific steam locomotives. While fewer examples of CPR steam avoided the torch (48) than was the case on Canadian National (71), the relative youth and technological sophistication of many CPR survivors secured for them an active and far-ranging "retirement" in the hands of tourist and museum operations in Canada and the United States.

Because of their advanced design and late construction, several members of the CPR's G5 Pacific class were revived in nostalgic operation on both sides of the international border. Initially preserved by F. Nelson Blount for his "Steamtown USA" operation, Nos. 1246, 1278, and 1293 all led active careers after retirement, as did Nos. 1201 (the last steam locomotive built by the CPR), 1238 and 1286.

Canadian Pacific itself, after sanctioning a number of "farewell" trips as steam's curtain fell, surprised the rail industry and its fans in 1998, when, at the behest of President and Chairman Robert Ritchie, the railway retrieved H1b Hudson No. 2816 from its longtime home at Steamtown and spent three years and $2 million restoring it to operation as a corporate ambassador. Dubbed "The Empress"—another iconic element resurrected from the CPR's storied past—the 4-6-4 has traveled widely in Canada and the United States.

While no Royal Hudsons are active at this writing, Nos. 2839 and 2860 have both enjoyed stints as mainline excursion power, the only semi-streamlined examples of Canadian Pacific steam to be revived, although other Royal Hudsons, as well as a pair each of F1a Jubilees and T2c Selkirks survive on static display.

OPPOSITE: Fresh from starring in the television serialization of author Pierre Berton's *National Dream*, A2m No. 136, along with D10h No. 1057, led an Ontario Rail Association excursion past a different breed of camera near Campbellville, Ontario, on May 5, 1974. Both locomotives remain in steam in 2006 on the South Simcoe Railway at Tottenham, Ontario. JOHN S. HOLLAND

ABOVE: Two Royal Hudsons have enjoyed post-retirement excursion careers. H1c No. 2839 ranged throughout the eastern U.S. in the late 1970s, and steamed through Allentown, Pa., on Feb. 5, 1979. ROBERT F. COLLINS, MORNING SUN BOOKS COLLECTION

INSET: Owned by the province of British Columbia, H1e No. 2860's second career kept it in regular excursion service over BC Rail trackage between North Vancouver and Squamish. AUTHOR'S COLLECTION

MONTREAL
Heart and Soul

Digging in for the short climb to Westmount, G3j Pacific No. 2467 leads Vaudreuil-bound suburban train No. 289 out of Windsor Station at 4:23 pm on August 19, 1958. The fortress-like structure facing Windsor Street (later renamed Peel St.), completed in stages between 1889 and 1954, was opened to regular traffic on February 4, 1889 and served as the Canadian Pacific's corporate headquarters for more than a century. Steam reigned supreme at Windsor Station for 60 years, until Alco RS-2 No. 8404 arrived from Newport, Vermont, with train No. 213 on September 13, 1949. This was the first use of a diesel on a scheduled train serving the terminal, and it was followed with considerable fanfare on December 9 of that year when the CPR's trio of brand-new E8A passenger diesels began leading their assigned B&M-CPR through trains to and from Boston's North Station. ROBERT F. COLLINS, MORNING SUN BOOKS COLLECTION

Considering Montreal's status as Canada's financial capital from before the time of Confederation well into the mid-20th century, it would have been remarkable had the Canadian Pacific Railway's founders chosen any other city to be its original headquarters.

Situated on an island in the St. Lawrence River, geography favored Montreal's development as a transportation crossroads. Adjacent rapids marked the westernmost limit of navigation for Atlantic shipping (and only then when the river was ice-free). Great Lakes shipping was likewise blocked from venturing into Montreal's harbor and farther downriver until the Lachine Canal bypassed the rapids in 1842. It was not until 1959, however, and the opening of the St. Lawrence Seaway, that large vessels could freely pass between the Atlantic and the Great Lakes. In the interim, Montreal had developed as a rail hub, and the city maintained this status even after the Seaway dimished its role as a transfer point between land and sea.

General offices, major shops, and freight and passenger terminals befitting a transcontinental anchor point were the most visible aspects of the CPR's presence in Montreal. When the first British Columbia-bound Canadian Pacific passenger train steamed out of Montreal on June 28, 1886, it departed from a modest depot near the city's harbor. By 1898, the CPR had erected a pair of imposing Romanesque structures to serve Montreal.

On August 19, 1958, train No. 181 departed Windsor Station for Ste. Thérèse behind G3h Pacific No. 2426. The burly 4-6-2 was a war baby, built by the Canadian Locomotive Company (CLC) at Kingston, Ont., in September 1944. CPR passenger locomotives built during the war had maroon paint omitted from their finish as a cost-saving move; many retained this simplified livery until retirement. BOTH, ROBERT F. COLLINS, MORNING SUN BOOKS COLLECTION

Place Viger, with its adjacent CPR hotel, was not far from the railway's original station, just east of what is today the historic district of Old Montreal. Windsor Station, completed in phases between 1889 and 1954 and incorporating the railway's general offices, was located some 1.5 miles to the west, but proved well-situated as the city's commercial core shifted in the same direction during the early 20th century. The CPR itself was part of that shift, vacating its former head office at 103 St. James Street on Place d'Armes. A third modern station, opened in 1931 on Park Avenue north of Mount Royal, saved passengers bound to and from Quebec City and Laurentian Mountain resorts a trip downtown to catch their train. By the time Place Viger hosted its last train in May 1951 (the hotel had already closed, but survives as a city office building), Windsor Station had long since become the CPR's primary Montreal passenger terminal.

A healthy commuter trade kept Windsor Station's platforms busy, while the arrivals and departures of the CPR's long-distance fleet leaders, from the celebrated *Trans-Canada Limited* of the 1920s to the *Dominion* and, finally, *The Canadian*, lent an aura of far-flung adventure.

Cross-border trains operated in conjunction with the Delaware & Hudson, New York Central, and Boston & Maine added more color to the CPR's Montreal-area operations even beyond the end of the steam era.

Appropriately, Windsor Station witnessed the final operation of Canadian Pacific steam locomotives in regular service, during the spring of 1960.

ABOVE: One of the last steam-powered trips out of Windsor Station was this April 17, 1960, "farewell" excursion to Smiths Falls, Ontario, led by H1b Hudson No. 2811. The CPR's last "official" steam run occurred on November 6, 1960, when A2q 4-4-0 No. 144 led an excursion marking the 75th anniversary of the driving of the railway's Last Spike. The cantilevered signal mast straddling No. 2811 in this view avoided blocking baggage wagon access on the narrow platform. GEORGE DIMOND

Vacated by their passengers and emptied of baggage and express, inbound trains backed out of Windsor Station to Glen Yard in Westmount. Known familiarly as "the Glen," the yard provided the day-to-day servicing needs of passenger rolling stock and motive power calling at Windsor Station. On March 29, 1958, H1c Royal Hudson No. 2821 left a vapor trail in its wake as it reversed through Windsor Station's throat trackage. ROBERT F. COLLINS, MORNING SUN BOOKS COLLECTION

ABOVE LEFT: Initially spawned by financial hardship experienced during the Depression, between 1933 and 1965 Canadian Pacific and Canadian National maintained a Pool Train Agreement aimed at reducing losses caused by duplicated passenger services in southern Ontario and Quebec. The majority of these "Pool Trains" operated between Toronto and Montreal. Among others were several runs between Quebec City and Montreal and one of these, No. 153, is arriving at Windsor Station with a typical pool-train mix of CPR and CNR rolling stock on August 19, 1958. Leading the *Frontenac* on this occasion is H1c Royal Hudson No. 2826, one of the first batch of 30 semi-streamlined 4-6-4s (Nos. 2820-2849) delivered by MLW in the latter part of 1937. ROBERT F. COLLINS, MORNING SUN BOOKS COLLECTION

LEFT: G5b Pacific No. 1229 bites into the grade leading out of Windsor Station as it heads train No. 173 to Ste. Agathe and the Laurentian district on March 29, 1958. A total of 102 G5 Pacifics were built between April 1944 and August 1948 as a modern design within traditional contours.

ROBERT F. COLLINS, MORNING SUN BOOKS COLLECTION

Henry Bowen served as the CPR's Chief of Motive Power & Rolling Stock from 1928 until his retirement in 1949. A steam stalwart, his mechanical legacy included semi-streamlined locomotives in three wheel arrangments; among these were a record-holding speedster and the last, and largest, steam locomotives built for a Canadian railway.

Early in his tenure as motive power chief, Bowen established a framework for the CPR steam roster that would endure until complete dieselization in 1960. Hudsons and Pacifics would be developed to handle most passenger assignments across the system, while those same Pacifics would share responsibilty for freight service with Mikados and, in the most challenging of western mountain grades, three subclasses of 2-10-4 dubbed Selkirks. The core of the CPR steam roster, however, would remain the 502 class D10 4-6-0s built between 1907 and 1913 and already well-entrenched across the system when Bowen took over responsibility for the road's motive power policies from his predecessor Charles Temple.

Bowen's semi-streamlining of 4-4-4, 4-6-4, and 2-10-4 wheel arrangements gave CPR steam a modern face, yet one that remained understated and dignified when compared to many contemporary efforts in the United States and Europe. Several subclasses of CPR Pacifics and Mikados built during the Second World War were given a hybrid front-end treatment that, while not as cleanly contoured as Bowen's Hudsons and their kin, still melded with what had by then become a distinctive "family" look at the larger end of the CPR roster.

Best remembered for his modern Pacifics and semi-streamlined power, Bowen also proposed several classes of CPR steam which were never built. Among these were a 2-8-4, a 4-8-4, and even a duplex-drive 4-4-4-4. And, while dieselization did not begin in a comprehensive way until after he had retired in 1949, the CPR's first forays into internal combustion occurred under Bowen's watch. Gas-electric cars were employed on branchline and secondary passenger schedules beginning in the early 1930s, and in 1937 the CPR placed in service its first diesel-electric locomotive. Boxy end-cab switcher No. 7000, built by a consortium of Canadian and British suppliers, paved the way for wartime Alco diesel switcher orders.

OPPOSITE TOP: These three views offer some lessons in CPR steam "comparative anatomy" as practised during the tenure of H. B. Bowen as the road's motive power chief. No. 2426 was a G3h heavy Pacific built in 1944 and delivered in the simplified passenger livery.

OPPOSITE BOTTOM: Built by CLC in March 1945 and differing most obviously in its maroon passenger scheme, G3h No. 2459 was equipped with an Elesco feedwater heater, rather than the Worthington model applied to No. 2426.

BELOW: H1c Royal Hudson No. 2821 shares No. 2459's paint scheme, but demonstrates how Bowen effected the cosmetics of his semi-streamlined styling with little more than minor sheet metal alterations to the jacket, pilot and smokebox front. ALL, ROBERT F. COLLINS, MORNING SUN BOOKS COLLECTION

ABOVE: G5b Pacific No. 1229 has been serviced and replenished at the Glen, and backs toward Windsor Station on May 29, 1957, as an MLW S-2 diesel switcher looks on. GEORGE DIMOND

BELOW: No. 2408, in its simplified livery, was a G3g Pacific built by CLC in late 1942. ROBERT F. COLLINS, MORNING SUN BOOKS COLLECTION

OPPOSITE TOP: G3j No. 2470 approached Westmount with an afternoon suburban run on May 29, 1957. GEORGE DIMOND

OPPOSITE BOTTOM: H1c Royal Hudson No. 2828 slows for the Westmount station stop en route to Ottawa with train No. 235 on May 30, 1957. GEORGE DIMOND

HUDSON ROYALTY

OPPOSITE TOP: More comparative anatomy, this time involving "standard" and semi-streamlined CPR Hudsons. H1b 4-6-4 No. 2816, at the Glen on May 9, 1959, wore the maroon-accented passenger livery as it was standardized after late 1935. Many road-service locomotives built in 1936 and later were given wide running-board skirts, eliminating the pinched effect fore and aft of the road number panel evident on older power like No. 2816.
ROBERT F. COLLINS, MORNING SUN BOOKS COLLECTION

OPPOSITE BOTTOM: H1c No. 2828 has just had its coal bunker topped off at the Glen in preparation for its next outbound trip on March 28, 1958. Mechanically, the "standard" and later semi-streamlined Hudsons were essentially identical. In order to achieve such a clean-lined boiler and smokebox silhouette, Bowen submerged a flattened sand dome beneath the boiler jacket, similarly hid the Elesco feedwater heater "bundle," replaced the steam dome with a steam-collecting pipe, and cleaned up extraneous plumbing and fittings.
ROBERT F. COLLINS, MORNING SUN BOOKS COLLECTION

Having made their debut in 1937, it was only fitting that one of Bowen's semi-streamlined Hudsons was selected to lead the 1939 Royal Train conveying Their Majesties King George VI and Queen Elizabeth over the westbound CPR portion of their landmark Canadian tour. Decorated to match the 12-car Royal Train in a livery of blue, black, and aluminum leaf, H1d No. 2850 also was fitted with a stainless steel boiler jacket, cast metal coats of arms on the tender and smokebox front, and cast crowns on the forward running board skirts.

No. 2850 led the Royal Train over the entire 3,224-mile CPR portion of its run, and so outstanding was its performance that the CPR sought, and received, permission from Buckingham Palace to call these engines Royal Hudsons.

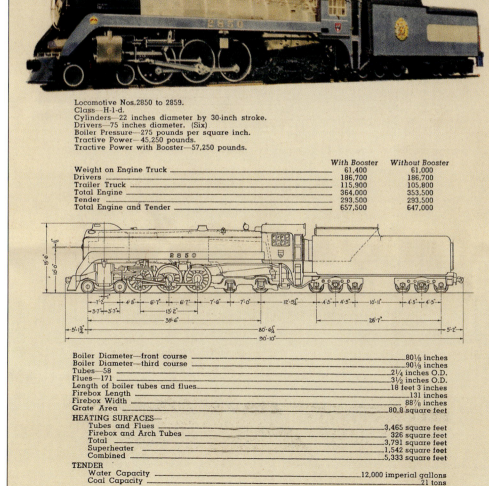

After completing its duties at the head of the 1939 Royal Train (assisted in the Rockies by T1a Selkirk No. 5919 and others), H1d Hudson No. 2850 was dispatched to the New York World's Fair along with Canadian National streamlined U-4-a Northern No. 6400, which had also led the Royal Train for part of its journey in Ontario. The CPR produced a fact-filled brochure for fairgoers, singing the praises of its soon-to-be Royal Hudsons and offering a rare color glimpse of No. 2850 in its Royal Train livery. Pilot train engine No. 2851, as well as western 2-10-4 helpers, retained their standard CPR colors during their stints on the 1939 tour. When Royal Hudson No. 2863 led a special train for Princess Elizabeth (the future Queen Elizabeth II) in 1951, it also kept its standard colors but was temporarily fitted with the stainless boiler jacket worn by No. 2850 for her parents' train in 1939.
AUTHOR'S COLLECTION

ABOVE: For decades, the CPR encouraged its station staff to tend gardens, originally for First World War food production and later for purely decorative reasons. Seeds and horticultural expertise were provided by the railway, and annual competitions were held to honor the best efforts. On August 13, 1954, G5a Pacific No. 1201—a ten-year-old product of the CPR's own Angus Shops and the last steam locomotive built by the railway—slowed for the Montreal West stop amid the station's blooms. GEORGE DIMOND

BELOW: Photographed at Montreal West on March 28, 1958, No. 1201's numerical double was a G3g Pacific turned out by CLC in October 1942. ROBERT F. COLLINS, MORNING SUN BOOKS COLLECTION

ABOVE: Flying white flags, G5b Pacific No. 1228 runs light through Montreal West on September 6, 1953. Although their appearance was a throwback to designs executed much earlier in the 20th century, Bowen fitted his G5 4-6-2s with such modern features as a welded domeless boiler; mechanical lubricator; HT-1 mechanical stoker; and a multiple front-end throttle. GEORGE DIMOND

BELOW: G5c No. 1258 heads train No. 248 out of Montreal West at 8:00 am on August 20, 1958. Fifteen minutes later, the morning commuter run from Rigaud would tie up at Windsor Station. The Pacific was a November 1946 product of CLC, and survived for 15 years until scrapping came in December 1961. ROBERT F. COLLINS, MORNING SUN BOOKS COLLECTION

27

ABOVE: No. 1258 again, this time leading train No. 213 out of Montreal West on March 28, 1958. Originating at Sutton, Quebec, near the Vermont border, this train served as an early morning all-stops local before crossing the St. Lawrence at La Salle and joining the Winchester Sub. at Montreal West for the last 4.7 miles into Windsor Station. BOTH, ROBERT F. COLLINS, MORNING SUN BOOKS COLLECTION

OPPOSITE TOP: Suburban train No. 246 from Rigaud stormed out of Montreal West on the same day behind G3j Pacific No. 2470. ROBERT F. COLLINS, MORNING SUN BOOKS COLLECTION

RIGHT: Train No. 232 was a morning Ottawa–Montreal schedule operating non-stop for the 106.7 miles between the nation's capital and Montreal West. H1c Royal Hudson No. 2828 has just completed that station stop and is accelerating the train towards Westmount and termination at Windsor Station on March 28, 1958. ROBERT F. COLLINS, MORNING SUN BOOKS COLLECTION

ABOVE: Photographed at Montreal West on August 20, 1958, G3h Pacific No. 2426 was delivered by CLC in September 1944. Bowen's heavy Pacific design featured 75-inch drivers and 22x30-inch cylinders, whereas the lighter but equally modern G5 engines were given 70-inch drivers and 20x28-inch cylinders. ROBERT F. COLLINS, MORNING SUN BOOKS COLLECTION

BELOW: G3j No. 2470 led a suburban consist at Montreal West on August 20, 1958. The ten-engine G3j subclass (Nos. 2463-2472) became the final heavy Pacifics acquired by the CPR. Delivered by MLW in June and July of 1948, they were also the last such locomotives built in Canada. ROBERT F. COLLINS, MORNING SUN BOOKS COLLECTION

G3j Pacific No. 2467 accelerates away from Montreal West with a morning suburban run on March 28, 1958. The CPR improved the lot of its commuter passengers in 1953, when 40 streamlined coaches were purchased from Canadian Car & Foundry. Each of the high-density cars sat 103 passengers, and was a marked improvement over prior generations of suburban equipment. ROBERT F. COLLINS, MORNING SUN BOOKS COLLECTION

OPPOSITE TOP AND ABOVE: On March 28, 1958, P1e Mikado No. 5162 led a westbound Extra freight through Montreal West. Built as P1b No. 5062 by MLW in August 1913, the 2-8-2 received its elevated subclass and road number in February 1928. ROBERT F. COLLINS, MORNING SUN BOOKS COLLECTION

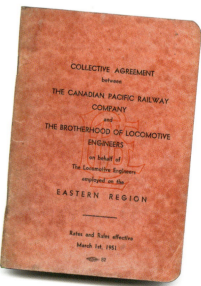

LEFT: Operating in suburban service, G3g No. 2408 occupied a junction track at Montreal West on March 28, 1958. The heavy Pacific was built in November 1942 by the Canadian Locomotive Co. at Kingston, Ont., and survived for the better part of two decades before scrapping in March 1961. ROBERT F. COLLINS, MORNING SUN BOOKS COLLECTION

ABOVE: With power from the CPR, New York Central, Delaware & Hudson and Boston & Maine passing through, dieselization was a particularly varied process to observers at Montreal West. On March 28, 1958, Ottawa-bound CPR train No. 233, behind an FPA-2/FPB-2, met inbound NYC train No. 25 from Malone, New York. ROBERT F. COLLINS, MORNING SUN BOOKS COLLECTION

BELOW: *The Canadian's* April 1955 debut bumped the *Dominion* to secondary status on the CPR's transcontinental run, and although the latter train did receive domes and other Budd equipment, its dieselized consists retained older maroon-painted cars like the 2200-series coach and heavyweight sleeper visible in this March 28, 1958 view of train No. 8 at Montreal West. ROBERT F. COLLINS, MORNING SUN BOOKS COLLECTION

BELOW: G5b No. 1229 leads train No. 180 out of Montreal West on March 28, 1958. With his G5 design, Bowen conceived a modern locomotive capable of freight or passenger assignment on virtually any part of the Canadian Pacific system. Intended, in large measure, to supplant the aged and obsolete D10 Ten-wheelers, the G5 Pacifics were themselves rendered obsolete all to soon as the tide of dieselization finally turned on the CPR. ROBERT F. COLLINS, MORNING SUN BOOKS COLLECTION

LEFT: G3g No. 2402—built by CLC in October 1942—had received maroon panels by the time of this March 28, 1958, view at Montreal West, just nine months before the 4-6-2 was retired that December and scrapped. ROBERT F. COLLINS, MORNING SUN BOOKS COLLECTION

RIGHT AND BELOW: G3h No. 2459 joined the CPR roster by way of CLC in March 1945. On the morning of March 28, 1958, the heavy Pacific was part of the parade of suburban runs—in this instance, train No. 270 from Vaudreuil—streaming through Montreal West on their way to Windsor Station. ROBERT F. COLLINS, MORNING SUN BOOKS COLLECTION

St. Luc Yard was opened by the CPR just west of downtown Montreal in July 1950, and has the distinction of being Canada's first modern hump yard. A state-of-the-art facility at the time of its construction, the inclusion of a large roundhouse—one of the last built anywhere in North America—was an anachronistic necessity to maintain the steam locomotives that were, at the time, still the mainstay of CPR freight operations.

St. Luc's opening saw the consolidation of many freight operations previously handled by older yards—Sortin, Outremont, and Hochelaga—located elsewhere in Montreal. Prior to St. Luc's construction, Sortin and Outremont yards had effectively split the role of the railway's main Montreal freight terminal, with Sortin, near Montreal West, fielding traffic to and from Ontario and western Canada as well as U.S. connections. Outremont, meanwhile, took care of most of the CPR's freight trains serving Atlantic Canada and Quebec from its location north of Mount Royal, and continued to play a diminished role after St. Luc's opening.

Roundhouses at Outremont and Hochelaga were closed when St. Luc's 37-stall facility was opened, making the new yard a magnet for CPR steam freight power in Montreal, and for fans eager to record them on film.

Steam and diesel locomotives await their next assignments at Montreal's St. Luc yard; in the distance is the roundhouse. Closest to the camera in this March 29, 1958, view are P1e Mikado No. 5163 and G2s Pacific No. 2541. ROBERT F. COLLINS, MORNING SUN BOOKS COLLECTION

TOP: G2s No. 2541 was a product of the CPR's Angus Shops, delivered in June 1908 as the railway's second No. 1141. It was rebuilt as G2d No. 2541 in 1913, and a further rebuilding in January 1924 saw the engine reclassified as a G2s. It was scrapped in December 1960, not quite two years after being photographed on the St. Luc ready line on March 29, 1958. ROBERT F. COLLINS, MORNING SUN BOOKS COLLECTION

ABOVE: Sister engine No. 2539 had followed a similar path to St. Luc that day, having been built at Angus in May 1908, but differing from No. 2541 most apparently in the application of an Elesco feedwater heater, with its distinctive "bundle" atop the smokebox. ROBERT F. COLLINS, MORNING SUN BOOKS COLLECTION

ABOVE: P1d No. 5114 was the subject of fans' attention at St. Luc on March 29, 1958. ROBERT F. COLLINS, MORNING SUN BOOKS COLLECTION

RIGHT: P2c No. 5343, at the St. Luc engine terminal on the same day, was built by MLW in November 1923, and served its owner until scrapped in November 1960. ROBERT F. COLLINS, MORNING SUN BOOKS COLLECTION

BELOW: Assigned to Kenora, Ontario, in the early 1950s, P2e No. 5369's graphited smokebox betrayed its recent status as a CPR "Western Lines" engine in this March 1958 view at St. Luc. Ft. William, Ont., marked the boundary between East and West on the Canadian Pacific. ROBERT F. COLLINS, MORNING SUN BOOKS COLLECTION

OPPOSITE TOP: N2b Consolidation No. 3692 is approaching St. Luc Yard in this August 11, 1954, view. GEORGE DIMOND

LEFT: P1d Mikado No. 5107 passes the tower at Ballantyne with a freight arriving from points west on the morning of August 13, 1954. GEORGE DIMOND

ABOVE: Also at Ballantyne—where CNR tracks crossed the CPR's "Lakeshore" route—G3g Pacific No. 2408 approaches St. Luc with an eastbound freight on November 23, 1956. GEORGE DIMOND

RIGHT: Outbound from Windsor Station beyond Montreal West, the CPR's Winchester Subdivision passed through the suburbs of Montreal's "West Island," also known as the Lakeshore. G5b Pacific No. 1229 led a commuter run at Grovehill on May 29, 1957. GEORGE DIMOND

BELOW: The low sun highlighting the contours of its smokebox door, G3g Pacific No. 2414 passed through Ballantyne with an arriving eastbound freight for St. Luc on August 13, 1954. GEORGE DIMOND

ABOVE: About to begin their daily trek to Windsor Station and downtown Montreal, commuters watch at Grovehill on November 24, 1956, as G5c Pacific No. 1264 brings their morning train to a halt. GEORGE DIMOND

BELOW: No. 1264's engineer awaits the highball. Over the next 7.6 miles he will repeat his pose at Montreal West and Westmount before completing his run at one of Windsor Station's bumping posts. GEORGE DIMOND

LEFT: Highball received, No. 1264 puts on a show as it departs Grovehill bound for Windsor Station on November 24, 1956. GEORGE DIMOND

OPPOSITE BOTTOM: An FA-1/FB-1 combination leading a long reefer block meets M4e 2-8-0 No. 3442 running backwards with a cut of stock cars near St. Luc Yard on November 23, 1956. GEORGE DIMOND

ABOVE: The *Dominion* was dieselized prior to the arrival of the Budd stainless steel cars ordered primarily for *The Canadian* and also used to selectively upgrade Nos. 7 and 8. Led by FP9A No. 1413 but with domes still a few months in the future, train No. 8 clipped through Valois near the end of its 2881-mile run from Vancouver on August 13, 1954. GEORGE DIMOND

BELOW: Near the opposite extreme of CPR passenger offerings at the time, G2s Pacific No. 2537 had a quintet of year-old streamlined suburban coaches in tow at Valois on August 13, 1954. GEORGE DIMOND

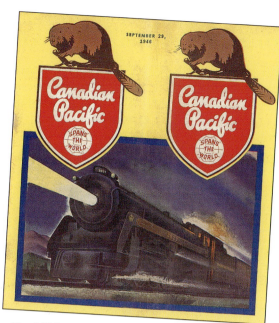

LEFT: H1c Royal Hudson No. 2828 breezed through Dorval with an Ottawa train on March 28, 1958. ROBERT F. COLLINS, MORNING SUN BOOKS COLLECTION; TIMETABLE, AUTHOR'S COLLECTION

OPPOSITE BOTTOM: G5a Pacific No. 1201 pulls away from Dorval station with what is likely Ottawa-bound train No. 235 on July 28, 1955. The CPR and CNR main lines parallel each other for much of their West Island mileage; the CNR's trackage is visible beyond the pole line at right. GEORGE DIMOND

BELOW: FPA-2 No. 4082 and an unidentified RS-10 lean into a curve past an opposing freight at Ste. Anne de Bellevue on July 28, 1955. St. Annes, as the CPR referred to the location in its timetables, marked the west end of both CPR and CNR trackage on Montreal Island. GEORGE DIMOND

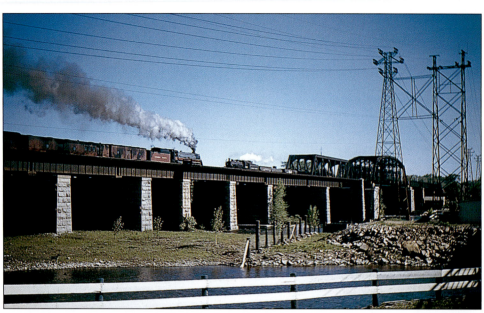
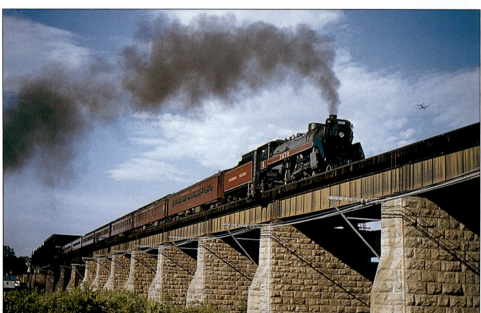

OPPOSITE TOP The CPR and CNR each maintained massive bridges crossing the Ottawa River near its confluence with the St. Lawrence at the west end of Montreal Island. With the CNR span in the foreground, two CPR passenger trains met on May 29, 1957. GEORGE DIMOND

OPPOSITE MIDDLE: G3j Pacific No. 2470 led a westbound suburban run at St. Annes on May 30, 1957. Just visible against the clouds at right is a Lockheed Constellation of CNR subsidiary Trans-Canada Airlines on approach to Dorval airport. GEORGE DIMOND

LEFT: G5a Pacific No. 1200 crossed the bridge at St. Annes on May 30, 1957. GEORGE DIMOND

ABOVE: AND RIGHT With F2a Jubilee No. 3004 dead in tow, G5b Pacific No. 1224 led an eastbound freight at Vaudreuil on March 28, 1958. BOTH, ROBERT F. COLLINS, MORNING SUN BOOKS COLLECTION

ABOVE: H1c No. 2828 was photographed departing Ste. Anne de Bellevue (St. Annes to the CPR) with a passenger train for Ottawa on May 30, 1957. GEORGE DIMOND

BELOW: G2u Pacific No. 2659 rushed a westbound Extra freight near St. Annes on May 29, 1957. GEORGE DIMOND

OPPOSITE TOP: At Vaudreuil on May 29, 1957, G5c No. 1257 (CLC, 11/46) and G3j No. 2472 (MLW, 7/48) exhibit the disparate lines of the CPR's final classes of Pacifics. No. 2472 was the last heavy 4-6-2 acquired by the railway. GEORGE DIMOND

RIGHT: G3j No. 2470, at Rigaud on May 9, 1959, was another MLW product of the summer of 1948, by which time the builder had shifted its focus to producing diesels under license from Alco. ROBERT F. COLLINS, MORNING SUN BOOKS COLLECTION

ONTARIO
Crossroads Contrast

P1e Mikado No. 5153 leads a Goderich Subdivision freight into Guelph Junction on May 15, 1958. Even at this relatively late date, Canadian Pacific steam had almost two years of revenue service left in Ontario before the curtain fell on April 30, 1960. Although many of the locomotives running out steam's final miles on the CPR were quite new—some as few as 12 years old—P1e No. 5153 was a definite veteran. Built by the Montreal Locomotive Works, the 2-8-2 entered CPR service in August 1913 as P1b No. 5053. At age 15, the engine was reclassified and had its original road number boosted by 100; the entire P1b subclass was similarly revamped between 1926 and 1930. ROBERT F. COLLINS, MORNING SUN BOOKS COLLECTION

Canadian Pacific never seemed to have the omnipresence in southern Ontario that rival Canadian National could claim, but that perhaps shouldn't be surprising for a railway that was originally built for the express purpose of linking Montreal with the Pacific coast. The logical, direct route west from Quebec bisected Ontario some distance north of the latter province's even-then heavily populated southern extremity, striking through the rugged Canadian Shield to the prairies and beyond.

It didn't take long, though, for CPR managers to set their sights on a share of southern Ontario's lucrative domestic and international traffic. They accomplished this goal largely through the acquisition of a patchwork of small railways, giving the CPR a network serving the region's commercial and industrial centers, with Toronto at the forefront. Access to U.S. connections, however, relied on the maintenance of a friendly relationship with the New York Central System. At the Detroit River, Canadian Pacific abandoned its short-lived car ferry arrangement in 1916 in favor of being permitted to move its traffic through NYC component Michigan Central's recently opened, electrified tunnel. Farther east, the CPR and NYC cooperated even more closely as joint owners of the Toronto, Hamilton & Buffalo Railway, an arrangement that gave Canadian Pacific much-coveted access to the Buffalo gateway.

The opposite extreme of the CPR's southern Ontario operations was a network of branches radiating northwest of Toronto.

LEFT: D10h No. 1059 worked near Ottawa on September 1, 1951. WILLIAM J. McCHESNEY, MORNING SUN BOOKS COLLECTION

MIDDLE: Recently returned to Montreal from New Brunswick and leading a November 22, 1959, CRHA excursion, A2q No. 144 made a photo pass at Williamstown, Ontario. ROBERT F. COLLINS, MORNING SUN BOOKS COLLECTION

BELOW: H1b No. 2811 was no stranger to the division point of Smiths Falls, Ontario, in regular service, and awaited its next departure on July 19, 1958. ROBERT F. COLLINS, MORNING SUN BOOKS COLLECTION

RIGHT: G1s No. 2219 had been turned out by the CPR's Angus Shops in Montreal during February 1910 as G1d No. 1019. Renumbered to 2219 in 1913, the engine was modernized in 1924, keeping its second road number but reassigned to subclass G1s. It mingled with diesels at Smiths Falls on April 17, 1960. ROBERT F. COLLINS, MORNING SUN BOOKS COLLECTION

PRECEDING PAGES AND BELOW: H1b No. 2811 made a farewell visit to Smiths Falls as part of a well-patronized and well-documented April 17, 1960, CRHA excursion from Montreal. Polished, if not pristine, for its sendoff, the Hudson took a spin on the turntable in preparation for the return trip. Looking on from within the roundhouse are representatives of some diesel classes that replaced the Hudson and its lesser stablemates. In the wake of the day's events, No. 2811 was retired and succumbed to the torch in December 1961. Sister engine No. 2816 was more fortunate. The only non-streamlined H1 to escape scrapping, it was sold to F. Nelson Blount in 1963, surviving at his Vermont "Steamtown USA" museum and that collection's mid-1980s relocation as the core of Steamtown National Historic Site in Scranton, Pennsylvania. Retrieved by Canadian Pacific in 1998 and restored to operation, No. 2816 again ranges across the CPR system. BOTH, ROBERT F. COLLINS, MORNING SUN BOOKS COLLECTION

RIGHT: M4a Consolidation No. 3408 started its career in November 1904, delivered by MLW as No. 1608. On July 19, 1958, the 2-8-0, outfitted with footboards and elevated back-up headlight, was well-equipped to handle yard and local duties at Smiths Falls. ROBERT F. COLLINS, MORNING SUN BOOKS COLLECTION

OPPOSITE BOTTOM: No. 2811 paused at Chesterville, Ont., during the April 17, 1960, excursion. ROBERT F. COLLINS, MORNING SUN BOOKS COLLECTION

RIGHT: **Smoking it up for lineside cameras, No. 2811 crosses the Rideau River and Canal at Merrickville, Ont., on April 17, 1960.** ROBERT F. COLLINS, MORNING SUN BOOKS COLLECTION

ABOVE AND LEFT: These two views of H1b No. 2811 were taken at Bedell, Ont., during the course of the April 17, 1960, CRHA excursion. Responsible for the design of this class of Hudson and later semi-streamlined examples, CPR Chief of Motive Power & Rolling Stock Henry Bowen also lent his hand to the distinctive, smooth-sided passenger equipment built, in part, by the railway's Angus Shops between 1936 and 1950. Produced in coach, sleeper, and several head-end plans, all were given welded sides with a gently curved cross section.
ROBERT F. COLLINS, MORNING SUN BOOKS COLLECTION

The rolling countryside around Toronto—Ontario's provincial capital and a major center of CPR and CNR operations—dictated that helper districts radiating from the city be maintained by Canadian Pacific until the end of steam. Helpers, manned by the "Cockney Pool" based at Lambton Yard in West Toronto, assisted trains north to Bolton, east to Leaside and Agincourt, and west to Orr's Lake, near Galt. The latter, at just over 55 miles, was the longest of the Toronto-based helper districts, and was required to surmount the Niagara Escarpment near Milton. Helper engines ran in front of the road power, and after cutting off at Orr's Lake backed the three miles to Galt where they were wyed for a more efficient return trip to Lambton Yard. On August 19, 1956, two members of the Cockney Pool—a name likely derived from their early colleagues' English heritage— meet the photographer's gaze as their 57-car westbound Extra climbs the Galt Subdivision's Milton Hill near Campbellville. On this trip, helper G1s Pacific No. 2224's fireman has provided a surfeit of steam as his charge leads P2f Mikado No. 5402. The engines' mechanical stokers are hard at work, evidenced by the steam plumes rising from both tenders. ROBERT F. COLLINS, MORNING SUN BOOKS COLLECTION

LEFT: Nos. 2224 and 5402 make what was likely a lasting impression as they continue their climb of the Niagara Escarpment near Campbellville on August 19, 1956.

OPPOSITE BOTTOM: Fans had a different perspective as this August 30, 1958, NRHS trip arrived at Guelph Junction behind G5c Pacific No. 1271 and H1c Royal Hudson No. 2839.

RIGHT: D10g Ten-wheeler No. 953 had eight cars in tow at Guelph Junction on March 21, 1959.

BELOW: G1s No. 2224 and P2f No. 5402 are just west of Guelph Junction on their August 19, 1956 climb to Orr's Lake. Double track from Toronto ended at the Junction.

ALL, ROBERT F. COLLINS, MORNING SUN BOOKS COLLECTION

G1s Pacific No. 2224 and P2f Mikado No. 5402 have roughly 20 miles left to go in their westbound climb to Orr's Lake as they depart Guelph Junction on August 19, 1956. No. 5402 had barely a year to go before it was scrapped in October 1957. Pacific No. 2224 survived a little longer, but met the same fate in February 1959. ROBERT F. COLLINS, MORNING SUN BOOKS COLLECTION

RIGHT: Guelph Junction marked the intersection, 39.2 miles west of Toronto Union Station, of the CPR's Galt Subdivision with the 111.8-mile Goderich Sub., the latter linking the port and heavy industry of Hamilton, on Lake Ontario, with the salt-producing port of Goderich on Lake Huron. P1e No. 5153 has arrived from Hamilton with a Goderich Sub. freight on May 15, 1958, and in this view occupies the Galt Subdivision's eastbound main track. Wyes on the Goderich Sub. north and south of the Galt Sub, along with crossovers on the latter, created a see-saw move for through Goderich Sub. trains, but avoided a diamond crossing here.

BELOW AND OPPOSITE BOTTOM: No. 5153 was built by MLW in 1913 as P1b No. 5053, and was reclassed and renumbered in 1928. The Mike has its tender cistern replenished from Guelph Junction's 40,000 Imperial gallon water tank on May 15, 1958. ALL, ROBERT F. COLLINS, MORNING SUN BOOKS COLLECTION

LEFT: Its work at Guelph Junction complete, P1e Mikado No. 5153 charges out of town on May 15, 1958, under a plume that is, hopefully, solely for the photographer's benefit. The 2-8-2 had 18 months left in the service of its owner before it was retired and scrapped in December 1959. None of the CPR's 160 P1 class 2-8-2s managed to escape the torch. ROBERT F. COLLINS, MORNING SUN BOOKS COLLECTION

ABOVE: No. 5153 negotiates wye trackage at Guelph Junction on May 15, 1958. ROBERT F. COLLINS, MORNING SUN BOOKS COLLECTION

BELOW: Craning for a clear view of the crew's hand signals, the Mikado's engineer backs his train toward Guelph Junction's 100-ton coal dock—just visible above the lead box car—and adjacent water tank. ROBERT F. COLLINS, MORNING SUN BOOKS COLLECTION

ABOVE: P1e No. 5158 departed Guelph Junction on August 19, 1956. ROBERT F. COLLINS, MORNING SUN BOOKS COLLECTION

RIGHT: On the same day, P2g Mikado No. 5405 led the 54 cars of train No. 70 east through Guelph Junction. P2 subclasses "g" through "k" were built by MLW and CLC between 1940 and 1948, following a 12-year drought of new Mikados joining the CPR roster. The very first of these modern Mikes, No. 5405 was received from MLW in July 1940 and, with its mates, was pressed into wartime service. This final wave of CPR 2-8-2 production shared the Bowen inspired front-end styling applied to the road's contemporary heavy Pacifics, G3 subclasses "e" through "j" of 1938–1948. ROBERT F. COLLINS, MORNING SUN BOOKS COLLECTION

ABOVE: A late-winter view of P2g No. 5405, leading train No. 86 at Guelph Junction on March 21, 1959. Sister engine No. 5411 had the distinction of powering the last regularly-assigned CPR steam run out of Toronto nine months later, on the last day of 1959. The last regularly scheduled CPR steam operation in Ontario occurred early the next year with N2b Consolidation No. 3722's April 30, 1960, departure from Port McNicoll. ROBERT F. COLLINS, MORNING SUN BOOKS COLLECTION

ABOVE: G1s Pacific No. 2214 led a westbound on the Galt Subdivision through Streetsville on July 19, 1959, headed for Guelph Junction and London. Streetsville was the junction of the Galt Sub's main line with the Orangeville Subdivision, which continued north beyond its namesake as the Owen Sound Subdivision and fed a collection of branches serving such rural communities as Walkerton, Fergus, Elora, Harriston, Wingham, and Teeswater. ROBERT F. COLLINS, MORNING SUN BOOKS COLLECTION

Canadian Pacific's Galt Subdivision runs 114.6 miles from Toronto to London; almost precisely halfway at mileage 57.2 is the Subdivision's namesake community (today part of the merged city of Cambridge). At Galt, the CPR interchanged with the Grand River Railway and the Lake Erie & Northern, both Canadian Pacific subsidiaries and both, through the end of the steam era, operated as electric lines. Passenger service on the GRR and LE&N had ended in April 1955, but freight motors still used the catenary visible in these three photos. In mid-1957 [ABOVE], G1v Pacific No. 2233 and P1d Mikado No. 5118 dusted the wires on their way past the CPR's Galt station with a westbound Extra freight. No. 5118, recently transferred from New Brunswick, performed some switching at Galt in the summer of 1957. AUTHOR'S COLLECTION

Canadian Pacific's southern Ontario mainline between Toronto and the important Michigan Central (NYC) connection at the Windsor/Detroit international border continued west of London as the 111.2-mile Windsor Subdivision. Just over 25 miles from the Detroit River was the community of Haycroft, where P1d Mikado No. 5118 was caught doing a bit of local switching before proceeding to Windsor in October 1959. Built at Angus Shops in October 1912, the 2-8-2 was renumbered in March 1926 and worked for over 34 years in this guise until retired and scrapped in September 1960. Even at the end of the steam era, this Canadian Pacific route saw a fair amount of passenger traffic; none of those trains, however, stopped at Haycroft. In the summer of 1958, for example, through coaches and sleeping cars were available between Toronto and Chicago on the *Chicago Express* and unnamed eastbound train No. 20 (the erstwhile *Canadian*, until that name was reassigned to the new Budd domeliner in 1955). Other schedules offered convenient connections at Detroit's Michigan Central terminal, where CPR Detroit trains terminated after being hauled through the MC's Detroit River Tunnel. Budd Rail Diesel Cars were introduced to several of the CPR's southwestern Ontario schedules beginning in 1953, displacing an earlier generation of speedster, in the form of F2a Jubilees Nos. 3000 and 3002, that were relegated to heavier weekend trains and backup protection on the route until 1955.

ALL, ROBERT F. COLLINS, MORNING SUN BOOKS COLLECTION; TIMETABLE, AUTHOR'S COLLECTION

H1c Royal Hudson No. 2827—its left-hand running-board crown missing—was in otherwise fine form at the head of this well-scrubbed consist in November 1959. EMERY GULASH, MORNING SUN BOOKS COLLECTION

BELOW: After 1916, Canadian Pacific traffic crossed the Detroit River via the Michigan Central's recently opened tunnel. The CPR maintained a waterfront presence, though, switching the Pere Marquette's (Chesapeake & Ohio after 1947) Windsor car ferry slips and shuttling cars to and from the PM/C&O yard in nearby Walkerville. With downtown Detroit in the distance, M4g 2-8-0 No. 3471 switches the Windsor slips on August 1, 1953. This operation ended in 1954 when C&O negotiated its own trackage rights through the tunnel. FRED AUSTIN, SANDY GOODRICK COLLECTION

AUTHOR'S COLLECTION

ABOVE: Running on Canadian National's Oakville Subdivision at Aldershot, Ont., with an eastbound Extra on May 17, 1958, CPR P2f Mikado No. 5397 was taking advantage of trackage rights dating to April 1896, when this Toronto–Hamilton line was operated by CNR predecessor Grand Trunk. The CPR 2-8-2 will run over the CNR as far as Canpa, 8.4 miles west of Toronto Union Station, where it will regain Canadian Pacific trackage for a dogleg north to the Galt Sub. and the last few miles into Lambton Yard. ROBERT F. COLLINS, MORNING SUN BOOKS COLLECTION

LEFT: D10e No. 839 worked through Waterdown, Ont., on August 9, 1955, with a ten-car Goderich Subdivision local freight. ROBERT F. COLLINS, MORNING SUN BOOKS COLLECTION

UPPER LEFT: As a Toronto-bound Canadian National freight drifts down the Dundas Hill into Hamilton West behind U-2-f Northern No. 6186, Canadian Pacific D10e 4-6-0 No. 839 smokes it up on the high ground of the Goderich Sub., heading north out of Hamilton on August 8, 1955.

LEFT: Canadian Pacific relied on its trackage rights over rival CNR's Oakville Subdivision to link its rails in Toronto's industrial west end with Hamilton, where the CPR's own Goderich Subdivision was reached, along with the ever-important connection to the Toronto, Hamilton & Buffalo Railway, a joint subsidiary of New York Central and Canadian Pacific funneling passenger and freight traffic to and from the international border at Buffalo. On August 8, 1955, CPR P2f Mikado No. 5403 led its 41 Hamilton-bound cars through the CNR's Bayview Junction.

ABOVE: H1d Royal Hudson No. 2840 leads train No. 741, one of the Toronto–Buffalo runs jointly operated by the NYC, TH&B and CPR. The train's consist in this October 7, 1954, view—not long after TH&B and NYC dieselized their portions of the run—included equipment from all three partners. The train is running over the CPR's Hamilton Subdivision on its last leg into Hamilton's TH&B station, having left the CNR's Oakville Sub. at Hamilton Junction and passed beneath the High Level road bridge (just out of view behind the train). TH&B trackage will take the train from Hamilton to Welland, where the New York Central will take over for the remainder of the run to Buffalo's Central Terminal. The 102.1-mile Toronto–Buffalo trip was scheduled to be made in three hours and 15 minutes; not a bad timing, but the parallel Queen Elizabeth Way highway (opened in stages after 1939 and considered Canada's first "superhighway") offered ever-more-competitive timing and had been siphoning away traffic for several years.

ALL, ROBERT F. COLLINS, MORNING SUN BOOKS COLLECTION

$\mathcal{A}$s a strategic link between "the two great systems"—those of owners Canadian Pacific and New York Central—the Toronto, Hamilton & Buffalo Railway loomed larger than its modest route mileage. Well past the end of the steam era, the TH&B offered a bridge route via southern Ontario's Niagara Peninsula for the freight and passenger traffic operating between the CPR at Toronto and NYC's Buffalo gateway.

Thanks to its TH&B connection, the CPR could offer Toronto passengers through-car access to schedules of the New York Central's storied "Great Steel Fleet." Thanks to locomotive pooling in place until the NYC and TH&B dieselized their portions of the Buffalo–Toronto passenger runs in 1954, NYC Hudsons regularly ran into Toronto Union Station, as did the pair of ex-NYC 4-6-4s acquired by the TH&B. After the NYC and TH&B legs were dieselized, the CPR retained steam on its Toronto–Hamilton portion of the run. Prior to 1954, those CPR locomotives that *did* run through to Buffalo (as well as TH&B power making the cross-border trip) had to be equipped with Automatic Train Stop equipment in order to run over New York Central trackage. Since this was non-standard gear for CPR power, a limited group of engines was fitted with ATS; over the final decade or so of CPR participation in the engine pool, these included G3d's Nos. 2332 and 2337, G2u's Nos. 2659 and 2662, G3g No. 2398, and G3j's Nos. 2465 and 2469.

The first Toronto–Buffalo through passenger train operated on May 30, 1897. By 1959, diesels had usurped the last pool assignments, with CPR cab units from General Motors and MLW replacing the Pacific and Royal Hudson holdouts. Consists continued to be an eclectic and colorful blend of equipment from the three pool partners, though, with maroon CPR and TH&B cars contrasting against NYC rolling stock clad in two-tone gray paint or stainless steel.

LEFT: H1d Royal Hudson No. 2856 chomps at the bit as its Buffalo–Toronto train waits at Hamilton's Hunter Street station on August 22, 1954. Conceived by the New York architectural firm of Fellheimer & Wagner—no strangers to NYC-related commissions—the terminal complex housed the TH&B's general offices as well as its Hamilton passenger station. Differing from a less-austere structure in the original 1930 proposal, the station's 1933 opening marked the first large-scale use of the emerging "International Style" of Art Deco-inspired architecture in Canada. Hamiltonians likely were more impressed with the massive grade-separation that was part of the new terminal's design, lifting the TH&B main line above downtown streets. ROBERT F. COLLINS, MORNING SUN BOOKS COLLECTION

BELOW: Leaving Hamilton behind as it skirts the westernmost reaches of Lake Ontario, G5c Pacific No. 1271 has just entered the eastbound main of the CNR's Oakville Subdivision at Hamilton Junction with Toronto-bound train No. 720 on August 8, 1955. To reach this point from Hunter Street station, the train has passed through the TH&B's downtown tunnel, run the length of the CPR's Hamilton Sub., passed under the High Level bridge (the stone-clad towers of which are visible at far right), and negotiated both the CPR's and CNR's respective Hamilton Junctions. ROBERT F. COLLINS, MORNING SUN BOOKS COLLECTION; TAG AND TIMETABLE, AUTHOR'S COLLECTION

A regular visitor to the Toronto, Hamilton & Buffalo Railway's Chatham St. roundhouse in Hamilton, Ont.—that's TH&B GP7 No. 74 resting in the shadows at right—Canadian Pacific G3j Pacific No. 2466 awaits its next trip on August 19, 1956. This locomotive was part of the last batch of heavy Pacifics built for the CPR; Nos. 2463–2472 were delivered from MLW in June and July of 1948. The 4-6-2 will lead a pooled NYC-TH&B-CPR passenger schedule to Toronto Union Station (via trackage rights over the Canadian National's Oakville Subdivision); by the time of this view, the two other pool partners had dieselized their portions of the Toronto–Buffalo route. ROBERT F. COLLINS, MORNING SUN BOOKS COLLECTION

ABOVE: G5c Pacific No. 1271 leads CPR Toronto–Hamilton local passenger train No. 732 out of Hamilton on August 9, 1955, having just passed through the short tunnel providing access to Hunter St. station. ROBERT F. COLLINS, MORNING SUN BOOKS COLLECTION

LEFT: P2f Mikado No. 5397 led a westbound freight into the TH&B's Aberdeen Yard in Hamilton on August 9, 1955. ROBERT F. COLLINS, MORNING SUN BOOKS COLLECTION

OPPOSITE TOP: P2g Mikado No. 5405 negotiates the CPR's Hamilton Junction trackage and is about to enter Canadian National's Oakville Subdivision on March 21, 1959. After employing CNR trackage rights for 28.9 miles, the 2-8-2 will regain CPR rails at aptly-named Canpa for the rest of its run to Lambton Yard in West Toronto. ROBERT F. COLLINS, MORNING SUN BOOKS COLLECTION

RIGHT: As the "van" of a CNR freight clears that road's Hamilton West junction on March 20, 1959, CPR P2g Mikado No. 5405 leads its own Hamilton-bound tonnage along the last few miles of the Goderich Subdivision. ROBERT F. COLLINS, MORNING SUN BOOKS COLLECTION

PRAIRIES
Spanning a Nation

Amid evidence of ongoing trackwork, G3f Pacific No. 2377 leads an Extra freight past the *Dominion* near Winnipeg in July 1952. The photographer's precarious vantage point for this view is the vestibule of one of the 35 streamlined coaches (Nos. 2200-2234) built by the CPR at Montreal's Angus Shops and placed in service beginning in 1948. A further 63 similar coaches followed (Nos. 2235-2297), the major distinction being ice air-conditioning on the first group and electro-mechanical cooling on the later cars. Both coach and Pacific were designed under the direction of the same man, Henry Bowen, the CPR's Chief of Motive Power & Rolling Stock from 1928 to 1949. WILLIAM J. McCHESNEY, MORNING SUN BOOKS COLLECTION

Between the "Lakehead"—the western limit of Canadian Great Lakes navigation, at the twin cities of Fort William and Port Arthur, Ontario, on Lake Superior (today's Thunder Bay)—and the Alberta foothills west of Calgary, Canadian Pacific's main line spans some 1,300 miles of mostly fertile prairie in southern Manitoba, Saskatchewan, and Alberta.

A network of branch lines grew to serve the agricultural needs of the region, funneling east toward Winnipeg where the CPR established what was for many years the largest complex of railway yards in the world. The CPR's mainline artery between Winnipeg and the Lakehead felt the seasonal passage of prairie grain destined for ships' holds and markets in eastern North America and Europe.

Although a widely held perception of Canada's prairies involves a flat, featureless landscape, the necessity for railways in the region to serve communities situated within deeply eroded river valleys ensured that, in steam days at least, helper districts were not restricted to the eastern and far western parts of the country.

The Lakehead, specifically Ft. William, also marked an important division within the CPR itself, for it denoted the boundary between the railway's "Eastern Lines" and "Western Lines." Differences between the two abounded, ranging from tastes in smokebox finish (graphite was the Western Lines' preference) to locomotive fuel.

LEFT: Between the farmland of southern Ontario and Quebec and the vast prairies of Manitoba, Saskatchewan, and Alberta, the CPR main line traverses the rocky, heavily forested Canadian Shield. Much of the CPR route north of Lake Superior vies with the western mountains for scenic appeal and operational hardship. This view of the *Dominion* near Nipigon, Ont., dates to July 1952; the normally-assigned Royal Hudson is being assisted by an FA-FB pair of MLW diesels. WILLIAM J. McCHESNEY, MORNING SUN BOOKS COLLECTION

With the petroleum industry figuratively exploding in Alberta in the immediate postwar years, cheap residual oil was embraced as a practical and cost-effective steam locomotive fuel by both the CPR and CNR. By 1950, 190 of the 900 steam locomotives assigned to the CPR's Western Lines were oil-fired. Although still in the majority, coal-fired engines were referred to disparagingly as "haystacks." Early conversions to oil fuel included the 16 Royal Hudsons assigned to Winnipeg–Calgary service; H1c's Nos. 2829-2837 and 2843-2849 were modified at Winnipeg's Weston Shops in 1949 and 1950.

The other half of the steam locomotive fuel equation—water—could be a problem on the prairies, so the CPR's Western Lines also adopted the habit of coupling an auxiliary water car behind steam locomotives destined for areas with particularly poor water quality.

BELOW: Graphite smokeboxes were a hallmark of CPR Western Lines steam power, as, to a lesser extent, were mahogany-hued cab doors. No. 2524 exhibits both characteristics at Winnipeg on May 2, 1953. ROBERT F. COLLINS, MORNING SUN BOOKS COLLECTION

TOP: Angus-built D10e No. 852 showed off its Western Lines appearance at Winnipeg on May 2, 1953. ROBERT F. COLLINS, MORNING SUN BOOKS COLLECTION

ABOVE: G3d Pacific No. 2343 was built by MLW in September 1926, late in the seven-year tenure of Charles Temple as the CPR's Chief of Motive Power & Rolling Stock. The 4-6-2 wore a black variant of the post-1936 passenger livery, as applied to older power, when it was photographed at Winnipeg on May 2, 1953. PRESTON JOHNSON

94

LEFT: G3d No. 2343 headed a line of dusty power at Winnipeg on May 2, 1953.
ROBERT F. COLLINS, MORNING SUN BOOKS COLLECTION

OPPOSITE BOTTOM: Trailing a water car, oil-fired G5b Pacific No. 1210 was the recent recipient of a thorough wipedown in this September 10, 1959, view at Winnipeg. The 4-6-2 was one of 30 G5b's (Nos. 1202-1231) built by MLW immediately after the Second World War.
ROBERT F. COLLINS, MORNING SUN BOOKS COLLECTION

BELOW: N2a Consolidation No. 3689, an MLW product of October 1911, was at Winnipeg on June 2, 1959.
ROBERT F. COLLINS, MORNING SUN BOOKS COLLECTION

RIGHT: Interestingly, more classes of CPR semi-streamlined steam power were assigned to the Western Lines at various times than was the case "back east." This, of course, was due to the construction of the T1b and T1c 2-10-4 Selkirks for mountain service in Alberta and British Columbia, and their subsequent demotion to freight duties east and north of Calgary. Still, examples of each of Henry Bowen's other semi-streamlined creations—H1 Royal Hudsons and both F1a and F2a Jubilees—were assigned to the prairies during steam's final decade. On May 3, 1953, oil-fired H1c Royal Hudson No. 2846 led train No. 7, the Montreal–Vancouver section of the *Dominion*, at Brandon, Manitoba. Stellar performers, a single H1c would routinely pull the *Dominion* between Ft. William and Calgary, an impressive 1,251 miles. ROBERT F. COLLINS, MORNING SUN BOOKS COLLECTION

BELOW: In 1952, fifteen of the 20 F1a 4-4-4 Jubilees were assigned to the Western Lines, and had by that time received a characteristic "stovepipe" extension to their original stack fairings, along with shrouded safety valves. Their Eastern Lines F1a counterparts got the stovepipe stack extension, but subsequently lacked the streamlined fairing. No. 2912 was at Winnipeg on June 1, 1953. PRESTON JOHNSON

OPPOSITE BOTTOM: F1a No. 2916 rode the Brandon turntable on October 5, 1957. The F1a class was built by CLC in 1937-38. Among improvements made by Bowen on the F1a's over his earlier F2a Jubilee design were smaller drivers (75- vs. 80-inch), an almost five-foot shorter wheelbase, and main rods connecting to the trailing driver. ROBERT F. COLLINS, MORNING SUN BOOKS COLLECTION

97

ABOVE: With the sun glinting off of its pale smokebox front, G5d No. 1273 simmered at Brandon, Man., on October 5, 1957. ROBERT F. COLLINS, MORNING SUN BOOKS COLLECTION

RIGHT: On June 8, 1959, G3h heavy Pacific No. 2435 was spotted outside the Souris, Manitoba, roundhouse. ROBERT F. COLLINS, MORNING SUN BOOKS COLLECTION

LEFT: D10k No. 1071 was at Souris, Man., on June 8, 1959.
ROBERT F. COLLINS, MORNING SUN BOOKS COLLECTION

MIDDLE: The auxiliary tender was a feature of CPR prairie operations, ensuring sufficient suitably treated water otherwise unavailable at online locations. D10g No. 926 was nearing its 48th birthday when it was photographed at Lac du Bonnet, Manitoba, on June 1, 1959. ROBERT F. COLLINS, MORNING SUN BOOKS COLLECTION

BELOW: No. 5781 was an R3d Decapod, the first of ten built as that subclass by Angus Shops in 1918-19. A total of 34 R3 2-10-0 engines (Nos. 5756-5790) emerged from Angus beginning in May 1917, augmenting an earlier group of R1 and R2 Decapods (Nos. 5750-5755) rebuilt there from 0-6-6-0s. Dividing its time between yard duties and helper service up from the floor of the Little Saskatchewan River valley, No 5781 was working at Minnedosa, Manitoba, on June 5, 1959, one year before the engine was scrapped.
ROBERT F. COLLINS, MORNING SUN BOOKS COLLECTION

Even late in the steam era, the operation of coal-fired locomotives persisted on the CPR's Western Lines. With the wipers not quite finished their day's work, G5c No. 1237 is coaled at Regina, the capital of Saskatchewan, on October 7, 1957. ROBERT F. COLLINS, MORNING SUN BOOKS COLLECTION

ABOVE: G3h No. 2438 was in good shape for its next trip at Moose Jaw, Sask., on June 4, 1959, with a brimming coal bunker and an auxiliary water car tagging behind.
ROBERT F. COLLINS, MORNING SUN BOOKS COLLECTION

RIGHT: Decapod No. 5762 was the highest-numbered member of the CPR's R3b subclass. The 2-10-0's crew obliged the camera at Moose Jaw, Sask., on September 3, 1959. The CPR converted six 0-6-6-0s into 2-10-0 Decapods soon after World War I as R2 class Nos. 5750-5755, and built new 2-10-0 engines as the R3 class between 1917 and 1919. All were intended to serve as helpers in the western mountains, but their rough-riding tendencies in road service quickly relegated them to yard and transfer duties, replaced as helpers by 15 new S2a 2-10-2s. ROBERT F. COLLINS, MORNING SUN BOOKS COLLECTION

H1c No. 2846, recently arrived from Brandon, Manitoba, via the CPR's Broadview Subdivision, pauses at Broadview, Saskatchewan, in June 1953 with train No. 3, the Toronto–Vancouver section of the *Dominion*. The Royal Hudson has led the train all the way from Ft. William, Ont., and will hand the consist over to a T1 Selkirk at Calgary. That semi-streamlined 2-10-4 will lift the *Dominion* through the Rockies and its namesake Selkirk Mountains before relinquishing the train to another Royal Hudson at Revelstoke, B.C., for the final leg to Vancouver. The *Dominion* was allotted a 15-minute stop at Broadview for servicing. This was enough time for passengers to take a stroll along the platform, but eastbound travelers venturing into town had to mind their watches—and porters' admonitions—as Broadview also marked the change between Central and Mountain time zones. PRESTON JOHNSON

MOUNTAINS
To the Coast

G4a Pacific No. 2709 leads train 11, the Medicine Hat (Alta.)–Vancouver *Kootenay Express*, west of Penticton, British Columbia, on May 5, 1953. Dieselization came early to the Canadian Pacific's Kettle Valley and Kootenay Divisions—together forming a secondary main line through the southern B.C. mountains—and scenes like this were a thing of the past by the end of 1953. ROBERT F. COLLINS, MORNING SUN BOOKS COLLECTION

With not one but *two* mainline routes traversing the western mountains between southern Alberta and the Pacific coast through the end of the steam era, Canadian Pacific was well positioned to meet the practical needs of shippers with this measure of redundancy. The railway also satisfied the more esoteric demands of passengers and tourists with some of the world's most breathtaking alpine scenery, from the vistas of Banff and Lake Louise on the "original" main line to the rugged confines of the scenic but operationally tortuous Kettle Valley line.

It was the Canadian federal government's promise of a railway spanning the prairies and crossing the mountains that convinced the people of British Columbia to throw their collective hats into the Canadian confederation. When Sandford Fleming first surveyed a Canadian Pacific route through the mountains, he opted for a passage through the Yellowhead Pass offering modest grades. The CPR's leadership favored a more southerly route, closer to the U.S. border, but requiring a far more challenging and expensive mountain crossing. Thus was the CPR bult west from Calgary via the Kicking Horse and Rogers Passes; Fleming's recommended route was later employed by CPR rivals Canadian Northern and Grand Trunk Pacific, both of which became components of the newly amalgamated Canadian National Railways in the early 1920s.

Engineering milestones like the Spiral Tunnels and five-mile Connaught Tunnel were completed early in the 20th century to

reduce gradient-related operational headaches dating from the main line's original construction, although several helper districts were still required well into the diesel era.

As expensive as CPR construction was along the railway's chosen mountain route, the ability to recoup some of those costs was seen in the unspoiled scenery through which track was being laid. Tourism and the CPR were firmly linked from the railway's earliest days, and it is no coincidence that Canada's greatest concentration of National Parks—including Banff, the first—lies astride the original Canadian Pacific main line.

With vacation travel poised to revive after the Second World War, Canadian Pacific resumed its prewar role as perhaps the pre-eminent promoter of Canada—and the Rockies, in particular—as a tourist destination without equal. The CPR's mountain resorts, crowned by the Banff Springs Hotel and Chateau Lake Louise and augmented by a range of affiliated properties advertised in the railway's timetables and brochures, were fed by a steady flow of passengers from the *Dominion* and, after 1955, *The Canadian*.

The DOMINION
CONDENSED SCHEDULES TRAINS 3-7 AND 4-8
Montreal-Vancouver Toronto-Vancouver
EFFECTIVE SUNDAY, APRIL 29th, to SEPTEMBER 29th, 1956 inc.
All Schedules are shown in Standard Time

Westward READ DOWN	Example	Altitude	Miles	Daily			Miles	Eastward READ UP	Example
No. 7								**No. 8**	
7.45PM	Sun.	109	0.0	ET	Lv......Montreal......Ar	ET	2881.3	9.35AM	Thurs.
10.00PM	"	215	111.4	"	Ar.......Ottawa......Lv	"	2769.9	7.25AM	"
10.20PM	"	215	111.4	"	Lv.......Ottawa......Ar	"	2769.9	7.10AM	"
1.30AM	Mon.	522	241.2	"	Ar.....Chalk River.....Ar	"	2540.0	3.45AM	"
4.50AM	"	662	358.5	"	Lv......North Bay......Ar	"	2522.8	12.20AM	"
6.35AM	"	857	437.5	"	Ar.......Sudbury......Lv	"	2443.8	10.30PM	Wed.
No. 3								**No. 4**	
10.30PM	Sun.	274	0.0	"	Lv.......Toronto......Ar	"	2703.6	7.00AM	Thurs.
6.15AM	Mon.	857	259.8	"	Ar.......Sudbury......Lv	"	2443.8	10.35PM	Wed.
No. 7								**No. 8**	
7.10AM	Mon.	857	437.5	"	Lv.......Sudbury......Ar	"	2443.8	9.50PM	Wed.
8.00AM	"	1378	471.5	"	Ar.......Cartier......Ar	"	2409.8	8.55PM	"
11.30AM	"	1411	607.9	"	Ar......Chapleau......Ar	"	2273.4	5.20PM	"
3.30PM	"	1223	737.8	"	Ar.....White River.....Ar	"	2143.5	1.50PM	"
7.00PM	"	996	956.1	"	Ar......Schreiber......Ar	"	2025.2	10.25AM	"
10.45PM	"	614	984.6	"	Lv.....Port Arthur.....Lv	"	1896.7	7.05AM	"
11.00PM	"	617	989.0	ET	Ar.....Fort William.....Lv	ET	1892.3	6.50AM	"
10.20PM	"	617	989.0	CT	Lv.....Fort William.....Ar	CT	1892.3	5.30AM	"
1.40AM	Tue.	1486	1136.2	"	Ar.......Ignace......Lv	"	1745.1	2.20AM	Wed.
5.05AM	"	1091	1282.4	"	Ar.......Kenora......Ar	"	1598.9	10.35PM	Tue.
8.05AM	"	766	1408.1	"	Ar.......Winnipeg......Lv	"	1473.2	7.30PM	"
10.00AM	"	766	1408.1	"	Lv.......Winnipeg......Ar	"	1473.2	6.45PM	"
1.15PM	"	1204	1541.2	"	Ar.......Brandon......Lv	"	1340.1	3.55PM	"
1.30PM	"	1204	1541.2	"	Lv.......Brandon......Ar	"	1340.1	3.40PM	"
4.45PM	"	1967	1672.1	CT	Ar.......Broadview......Lv	CT	1209.2	12.50PM	"
3.55PM	"	1967	1672.1	MT	Lv.......Broadview......Ar	MT	1209.2	11.40AM	"
6.05PM	"	1896	1764.5	"	Ar.......Regina......Lv	"	1116.8	9.40AM	"
6.25PM	"	1896	1764.5	"	Lv.......Regina......Ar	"	1116.8	9.20AM	"
7.20PM	"	1778	1806.1	"	Ar.....Moose Jaw.....Lv	"	1075.2	8.25AM	"
7.50PM	"	1778	1806.1	"	Lv.....Moose Jaw.....Ar	"	1075.2	7.50AM	"
10.40PM	"	2432	1916.5	"	Ar.....Swift Current.....Lv	"	964.8	5.30AM	"
10.55PM	Wed.	2432	1916.5	"	Lv.....Swift Current.....Ar	"	964.9	5.15AM	"
2.40AM	Wed.	2181	2064.9	"	Ar.....Medicine Hat.....Lv	"	816.4	1.45AM	"
3.00AM	"	2181	2064.9	"	Lv.....Medicine Hat.....Ar	"	816.4	1.30AM	Tue.
8.00AM	"	3438	2239.7	"	Ar.......Calgary......Lv	"	641.6	9.25PM	Mon.
8.50AM	"	4338	2239.7	"	Lv.......Calgary......Ar	"	641.6	8.55PM	"
11.20AM	"	4534	2321.6	"	Ar.......Banff......Lv	"	559.7	6.40PM	"
11.30AM	"	4534	2321.6	"	Lv.......Banff......Ar	"	559.7	6.30PM	"
12.30PM	"	5050	2356.3	"	Ar.....Lake Louise.....Lv	"	525.0	5.40PM	"
1.30PM	"	4072	2376.3	MT	Ar.......Field......Lv	MT	505.0	4.35PM	"
12.40PM	"	4072	2376.3	PT	Lv.......Field......Ar	PT	505.0	3.25PM	"
2.50PM	"	2583	2411.2	"	Ar.......Golden......Lv	"	470.0	2.00PM	"
6.20PM	"	1494	2502.0	"	Ar.......Revelstoke......Lv	"	379.3	10.20AM	"
6.40PM	"	1494	2502.0	"	Lv.......Revelstoke......Ar	"	379.3	10.00AM	"
8.05PM	"	1153	2546.0	"	Ar.......Sicamous......Lv	"	335.2	8.20AM	"
8.15PM	"	1153	2546.0	"	Lv.......Sicamous......Ar	"	335.2	8.10AM	"
11.00PM	"	1159	2630.8	"	Ar.......Kamloops......Lv	"	250.5	5.25AM	"
11.10PM	"	1159	2630.8	"	Lv.......Kamloops......Ar	"	250.5	5.15AM	"
4.00AM	Thur.	493	2753.3	"	Ar.....North Bend.....Lv	"	129.0	12.35AM	Mon.
4.10AM	"	493	2753.3	"	Lv.....North Bend.....Ar	"	129.0	11.55PM	Sun.
6.09AM	"	59	2811.1	"	Ar.......Agassiz......Lv	"	70.1	9.55PM	"
8.30AM	"	14	2881.3	PT	Ar.......Vancouver......Lv	PT	0.0	8.00PM	Sun.

ABOVE: G3g Pacific No. 2386 arrives at Calgary station (a portion of which is visible to the right of the engine's smokebox) with eastbound train No. 2 on September 12, 1949. At this time, No. 2 and its opposite, No. 1, were unnamed maids of all work making virtually every stop on their Vancouver–Montreal treks, arriving in Calgary at half-past noon with coaches, sleepers, a buffet-parlor and plenty of head-end traffic from Vancouver. The tall structure rising above the train is the CPR's Hotel Palliser. SANDY GOODRICK

RIGHT: Near Banff, Alta., from the westbound *Dominion* in September 1949. SANDY GOODRICK

ABOVE: Looking back from the rear platform of train No. 7 at Morley, Alberta, on September 12, 1949, where a pair of westbound freights has taken siding for the *Dominion's* passage. SANDY GOODRICK

RIGHT: Led by a T1 Selkirk, the westbound *Dominion* follows the course of the Bow River near Banff on September 12, 1949. In addition to a 2100-series and wide-windowed 2200-series streamlined coach duo running Montreal–Vancouver, the otherwise heavyweight consist of the period included a healthy mix of sleepers, mostly 12-1s and mostly running right through from Montreal to Vancouver. A Winnipeg–Vancouver 12-1 and a Regina–Vancouver 13-section tourist sleeping car catered to the needs of intermediate riders, as did a Winnipeg–Vancouver colonist car. A dining car was added at Medicine Hat, Alta., for the balance of the trip to the Pacific coast (the previous diner having been removed at Swift Current, Saskatchewan). SANDY GOODRICK

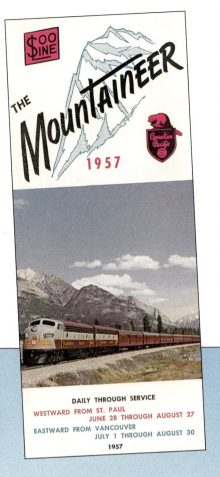

The *Mountaineer* was a summer-only through train operated to tap the Chicago and Twin Cities markets in conjunction with CPR subsidiary Soo Line. Like the year-round *Soo-Dominion* schedule, the *Mountaineer* crossed the border at Portal, N.D.-N. Portal, Sask., and employed a connection with the CPR main line at Moose Jaw. To the west lay the well-advertised splendors of the CPR's mountain resorts.
AUTHOR'S COLLECTION

ABOVE: P2j Mikado No. 5443 was caught from the westbound *Dominion's* rear platform near Lake Louise, Alberta, on September 12, 1949. SANDY GOODRICK

BELOW: Canadian Pacific spared little expense in the production of brochures, maps, guide books and posters, from the company's earliest years well into the 1950s, and many of the most attractive publications dealt, not surprisingly, with one of the CPR's most valuable "assets"—the stunning mountain scenery flanking its main line. This 1937 offering showcased the Banff Springs Hotel. AUTHOR'S COLLECTION

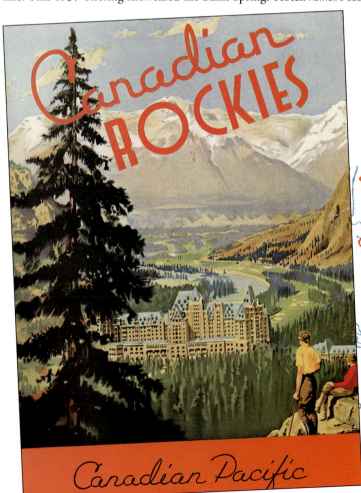

RIGHT: At Lake Louise, another P2j Mikado prepared to head west behind the *Dominion* on September 12, 1949. Ahead lay the final 5.6 miles of the climb to Stephen, marking the summit of the Continental Divide and the Alberta-British Columbia border. SANDY GOODRICK

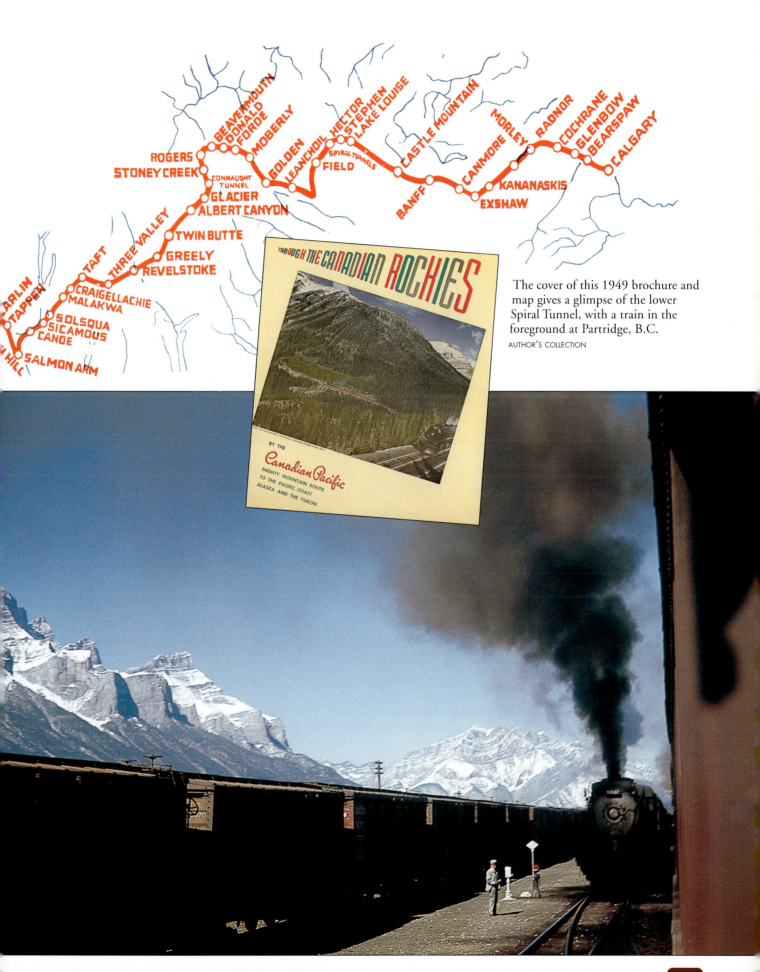

The cover of this 1949 brochure and map gives a glimpse of the lower Spiral Tunnel, with a train in the foreground at Partridge, B.C.
AUTHOR'S COLLECTION

Having just completed its climb of the "Big Hill" via the Spiral Tunnels—cresting the Continental Divide at Stephen—nine-year-old T1b Selkirk No. 5922 paused at Lake Louise in September 1947. Eighteen months later, No. 5922 and its nine T1b classmates were joined in their mountain assignments by Canada's last new steam power, six members of the CPR's T1c class, delivered by MLW in February and March 1949 as Nos. 5930-5935. The semi-streamlined Selkirks' employment on the Laggan and Mountain Subdivisions was soon at an end, however. General Motors F-units dieselized freight trains between Calgary and Revelstoke in 1951, and by the end of 1952 steam on passenger trains had also succumbed. The displaced Selkirks, including members of the original, non-streamlined T1a subclass of 1929, were reassigned to freight service between Calgary and Swift Current, Sask., as well as Calgary–Edmonton; the Selkirks bumped various classes of Pacifics from these runs, permitting elimination of several helper districts and effecting annual operating savings of over a half-million dollars. Of considerable interest in this 1947 photograph are the two portable auxiliary lights flanking the recessed main headlight. This is one of the earliest documented applications of what would become known as "ditch lights"—the two beams were aimed to cross, providing a wide swath of light by which crews could more easily spot fallen rocks and other obstructions on twisting mountain trackage. As standard power on CPR passenger trains between Calgary and Revelstoke after 1938, the semi-streamlined Selkirks were given a high profile in company advertising and promotional literature. The cover of a 1949 route guide featured westbound T1b No. 5925 entering the lower Spiral Tunnel. DR. HOWARD BLACKBURN; MORNING SUN BOOKS COLLECTION; BROCHURE, AUTHOR'S COLLECTION

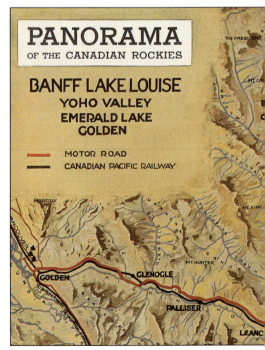

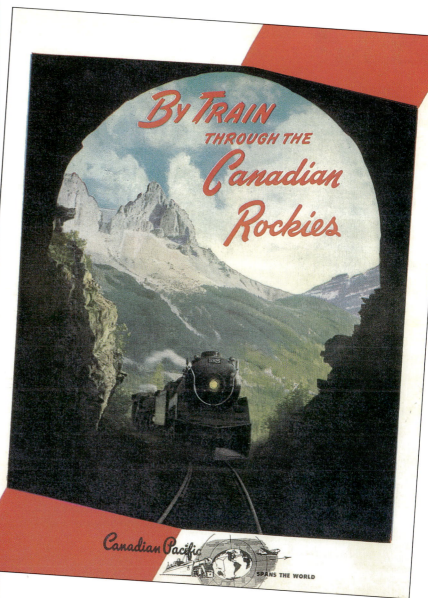
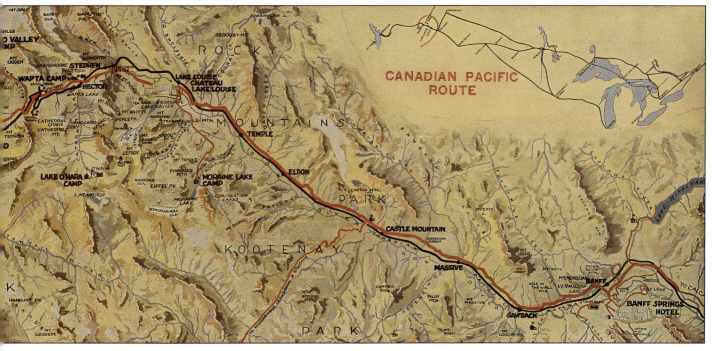

ABOVE: G3f Pacific No. 2371 paused at Lethbridge, Alta., on May 4, 1953, with train No. 68, an all-stops overnight run from Nelson, B.C. to Medicine Hat via the Kootenay Division. The train's consist has been switched prior to starting on the last leg of its trip east.
ROBERT F. COLLINS, MORNING SUN BOOKS COLLECTION

RIGHT: Assigned to train No. 11, the *Kootenay Express*, G3g No. 2386 was also at the CPR's Lethbridge station that day. Both heavy Pacifics were built by MLW in the spring of 1940.
ROBERT F. COLLINS, MORNING SUN BOOKS COLLECTION

Providing a somewhat less-than-direct alternate link between southern Alberta and Vancouver through the end of the steam era was Canadian Pacific's so-called "second main line."

Bridges, tunnels, grades and curves abounded here—the combined Crowsnest and Kettle Valley route between Medicine Hat, Alta., and the Pacific coast. It was the strength of lucrative mineral, forest product, and other on-line traffic, more than perennially thin through service, that kept this southerly CPR route open during winters that could deposit 30 or more *feet* of snow on the Kettle Valley line's Coquihalla Pass by the time spring finally arrived. The Kootenay Division comprised the eastern half of the route, reaching B.C. via the Crowsnest Pass. The Kettle Valley Division ran to a mainline connection at Odlum (Hope), British Columbia. With the Kootenay Division virtually complete by 1898, and the Kettle Valley operation in place by the First World War, it wasn't until 1930, when the last gap between Kootenay Landing and Nelson was built, that through train service was possible, replacing a steamboat connection on Kootenay Lake.

Steam disappeared from these lines by the end of 1953, displaced by a targeted plan that saw 73 new diesels—F-M/CLC units on passenger and an initial mix of MLW and GMD power in freight and yard duty—replace the 92 steam locomotives (81 of which were oil-fired) holding down the route's assignments at the time. Over half of these were N2 Consolidations, with a mix of P1 Mikados, M4 Consolidations, D10 Ten-wheelers, R3 Decapods, and various Pacifics.

BELOW: Passengers milled on May 4, 1953, as Kootenay Division train No. 11, the Medicine Hat–Vancouver *Kootenay Express*, stopped at Crowsnest, 111 miles west of Lethbridge. Crowsnest marked the crossing of the Continental Divide on this CPR route, the Alberta-B.C. border, and the demarcation between the Mountain and Pacific time zones. The station, shown in the westward-facing view, was just west of the Divide. PRESTON JOHNSON

While Kootenay Division train No. 11, the *Kootenay Express*, (at right) made its Crowsnest station stop on May 4, 1953, eastbound P1e Mikado No. 5148 was attended to in the Crowsnest yard. Another P1e is visible in the distance, near the coal dock on the yard's south side. Coal was, and remains, an important part of the Crowsnest-area economy, providing much of the traffic passing through the yard. Following its 15-minute stop, train No. 11 will depart at 11:25 am Pacific Time, behind G3f Pacific No. 2375, for the continuation of its 962.3-mile, almost 38-hour journey between Medicine Hat and Vancouver. Slow operation across the Kootenay and Kettle Valley Divisions meant that most time-sensitive traffic between Alberta and the Pacific coast went via the original main line through Banff, Lake Louise, and

Revelstoke. On-line freight and passenger business kept the "second" main line in business, although all-rail through service was possible only after 1930, when tracks finally were completed between Kootenay Landing and Nelson. Prior to this, steamboats were employed to make the connection. At the time of this photograph, heavy G3 Pacifics typically handled the route's through passenger trains between Medicine Hat and Nelson, in order to cope with seasonal head-end business, mostly in the form of tree-fruit shipments; other times of the year, lighter G2 Pacifics were adequate. West of Nelson on the Kettle Valley Division, stablemates of the P1 engines visible here usually led the passenger trains prior to diesels taking over in mid-1953.
ROBERT F. COLLINS, MORNING SUN BOOKS COLLECTION

RIGHT: While Banff, on the original main line, was certainly worthy of its high profile in CPR advertising, Cranbrook, British Columbia's mountain backdrop is no less impressive. With its displacement by F-M/CLC C-Line passenger diesels imminent, G3f 4-6-2 No. 2375 awaited the continuation of its run towards Vancouver with the *Kootenay Express* on May 4, 1953. PRESTON JOHNSON

BELOW: At Penticton, B.C., G4a Pacific No. 2709 runs light through the yard on May 5, 1953, prior to leading train No. 11 west. The string of refrigerator cars at left reflects Penticton yard's role as a gathering point for traffic generated by the bountiful orchards of the Okanagan Valley. ROBERT F. COLLINS, MORNING SUN BOOKS COLLECTION

OPPOSITE BOTTOM: P1n Mikado No. 5250, photographed at Penticton on May 5, 1953, was one of 65 locomotives (Nos. 5200-5264) rebuilt by the CPR from obsolete N2 Consolidations between September 1946 and December 1949. No. 5250 was built by MLW in November 1912 as N3b No. 3918. It was reconfigured as N2b No. 3718 in August 1929, and emerged as 2-8-2 No. 5250 in June 1949. PRESTON JOHNSON

ABOVE: G4a Pacific No. 2709—an Angus Shops product of March 1920—led train No. 11 at Princeton, B.C., on May 5, 1953, in the last months of steam operation on the CPR's Kettle Valley District. ROBERT F. COLLINS, MORNING SUN BOOKS COLLECTION

OPPOSITE TOP: Heavy snow on the Kettle Valley's Coquihalla Pass—as much as 30 or 40 *feet* over a winter—was an extreme operating impediment and, as a source of runoff-induced washouts, spelled the line's demise beginning in 1959 when the Odlum (Hope)–Brodie segment was closed. In this May 5, 1953, scene at the Coquihalla station, locals are already in shirtsleeves with plenty of winter's legacy left to melt. ROBERT F. COLLINS, MORNING SUN BOOKS COLLECTION

RIGHT: Train No. 12, the *Kettle Valley Express*, runs behind double-headed power at Coquihalla on May 5, 1953. P1n Mikado No. 5261—another former 2-8-0, rebuilt in September 1949—pilots N2a Consolidation No. 3639, many of whose stablemates became fodder for the 2-8-2 conversions. ROBERT F. COLLINS, MORNING SUN BOOKS COLLECTION

ABOVE: Although it spent much of its later career in the relative obscurity of Sicamous–Kelowna, B.C., local service, D10j No. 962 was very much a celebrity, at least to those with a knowledge of the CPR's locomotive painting practices. The otherwise unassuming D10 was given passenger-service maroon panels when it led an inspection train operated for CPR Chairman and President W. M. Neal in 1947. Unlike the various other power spiffed up for the system-wide event, No. 962 retained its special livery. In this view, the well-polished 4-6-0 was holding down its customary assignment as it prepared to depart Sicamous, B.C., for Kelowna in July 1952. The train served the fertile Okanagan Valley, famous for its apples and other tree fruit; the well-ventilated express car leading the consist served this lucrative market. WILLIAM J. MCCHESNEY, MORNING SUN BOOKS COLLECTION

RIGHT: Deep in the Fraser River valley at Agassiz, B.C., H1e Royal Hudson No. 2863 was 309 miles into its Revelstoke-to-Vancouver trip at the head of train No. 7, the Montreal–Vancouver section of the *Dominion*, on September 13, 1949. Vancouver's downtown terminal lay just 70 miles and two hours ahead. Unlike members of earlier semi-streamlined H1 subclasses that were reconfigured as oil-burners in 1949-50, the five H1e's of June 1940—the last Royal Hudsons built—were oil-fired right from the MLW factory, as they were intended specifically for the Revelstoke–Vancouver assignment. After the Second World War, the CPR shifted the emphasis of its trans-Pacific services from steamships to airliners, although passengers detraining at Vancouver could still make a convenient connection to the CPR's coastal *Princess* steamers. SANDY GOODRICK

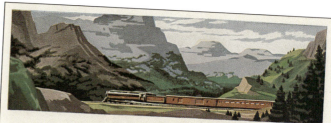

ABOVE: M4e Consolidation No. 3448 clatters east through New Westminster, B.C., on September 6, 1950. The engine was built at the railway's Angus Shops in June 1906 as No. 1648, becoming No. 3448 as part of a comprehensive system renumbering undertaken in 1912-13. The veteran 2-8-0 had almost exactly five years of service remaining at the time of this view; it was retired and scrapped in September 1955. New Westminster, southeast of the CPR's downtown Vancouver terminals, was reached by a branch built in the first decade of the 20th century. Canadian Pacific trains shared the route with lessor British Columbia Electric Railway; a BCER electric suburban car can be seen in the distance at far left. SANDY GOODRICK

RIGHT: In the early 1950s, V4a 0-8-0 No. 6939 was assigned to Tadanac, B.C., where it switched the Trail smelter of CPR subsidiary Consolidated Mining & Smelting Company. The compact headlight reflected the 0-8-0's erstwhile employment in Vancouver, where, converted to oil fuel, it was photographed circa 1950. It emerged from MLW in September 1908 as M4h Consolidation No. 1734, becoming No. 3534 in August 1912 as part of the CPR's major system renumbering. Conversion from 2-8-0 to 0-8-0 came in July 1928; a total of 30 Consolidations were rebuilt as switchers in this fashion between May 1928 and November 1929, becoming V4a's Nos. 6920-6949. AUTHOR'S COLLECTION